Cooking
with the
World's Best

melbourne
food & wine
festival

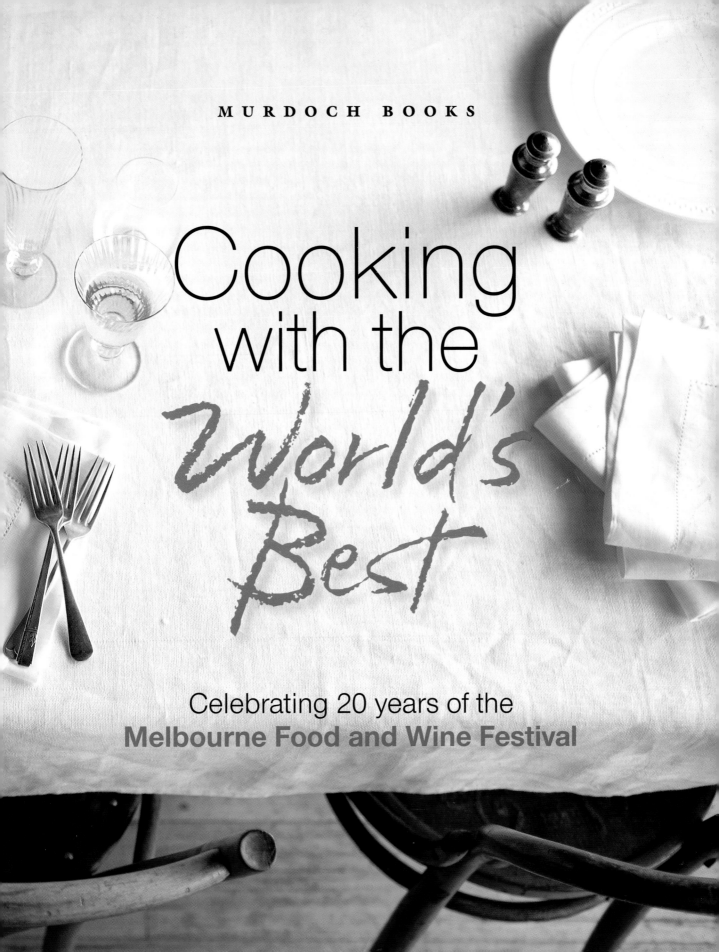

MURDOCH BOOKS

Cooking with the *World's Best*

Celebrating 20 years of the
Melbourne Food and Wine Festival

Swing in Manchester Lane Event, 2009.

Contents

Foreword

Started by Peter Clemenger, AM, from grassroots 20 years ago, Melbourne Food and Wine Festival's growth and success is a tribute to the energy, passion and innovation of Victoria's food and wine industries. Each March, the Festival holds a mirror up to the state's world-class food and wine culture and the global trends of the day.

As Melbourne Food and Wine Festival Chairman since 2004, my greatest satisfaction has been to witness the evolution of a "nice little program" — as some close to the Festival referred to this celebration in its early days — into what is now an all-embracing, award-winning hallmark event on the Victorian calendar.

The Festival team is incredibly privileged to work with enthusiastic sponsors, government and media partners, through to countless behind-the-scenes volunteers, without whom this special celebration would not be possible.

Happy 20th anniversary!

John Haddad, AO
Chairman, Melbourne Food and Wine Festival

Night of the Coq, Libertine, 2009.

Introduction

Let the Feasting Begin

It seems fitting that Melbourne, a city with an almost pathological devotion to the art of eating and drinking, should host one of the world's great food and wine festivals. This is, after all, a town that boasts seven long-running, much-loved produce markets, is surrounded on all sides by wine-producing regions, whose supporters discuss the finer points of restaurant meals with the passion of sports fanatics, get hot under the collar arguing about where to get the best pizza or dim sum and are ready to cross town to source bread or pork or cheese. It's a city that believes ready access to an excellent glass of wine is one of the secrets to a good life and that the joys of talking about food and wine are secondary only to consuming it.

Two decades since the Melbourne Food and Wine Festival made its debut, it's now hard to imagine March in Melbourne without the company of the world's best chefs and winemakers, without the classes and tastings, demonstrations and lectures, tours and special dinners, without the 400,000 other food fanatics who turn out to participate in more than 300 separate events that span the city and the state. March has become the month when the Festival holds a mirror up to Melbourne to reflect and celebrate one of the city's great and most unique strengths.

The Chicago Tribune voted this particular festival as one of the five things you should do before you die. DAMIEN PIGNOLET, 2009

It's hard to reconcile the size and scope of the Melbourne Food and Wine Festival today with the fledgling 1993 version that produced about 10 events, some of which struggled to attract a crowd. But part of the reason that the Festival survived and now stands out on an increasingly crowded calendar of similar festivals world-wide, is that it has stuck with the same independent, inclusive and un-ashamedly idealistic spirit that brought the initial event into being. There's been a firm commitment to both engage with the local industry and to include as many free events as possible to attract the largest number of people from outside of the industry.

Then there's the way the invited talent is treated. To this day, the Festival sticks to the strict policy of paying all guests the same fee (an airfare and an honorarium) no matter what their level of stardom — or number of stars — and is adamant that every Festival guest should be whisked around Melbourne, plied with all of its greatest food and alcohol and be shown the best time possible. An invitation to the Melbourne Food and Wine Festival has become synonymous with an invitation to a good time.

But just as the Festival involves a certain amount of merriment it's also deadly serious when it comes to food and wine. How else to explain the roll call of guests that has included Charlie Trotter and Anthony Bourdain, Elena Arzak and René Redzepi, Stephanie Alexander and Neil Perry, Heston Blumenthal and Mario Batali, Madhur Jaffrey and Henri Krug? Why else would the Festival champion organics and biodynamics, farmers' markets, Slow Food, regionality, terroir, sustainability, food ethics, artisan producers and foraging before it

became fashionable to do so? And how else to explain the way the Festival has shone light on Melbourne's, and Victoria's, most recognisable assets — the wine regions, the produce markets, the city's laneways and rooftops, the coffee and bar cultures — bringing them to the attention of a wider audience?

The answers are that the Melbourne Food and Wine Festival, like the city it calls home, is truly interested in this stuff.

> There is a groundswell of people that absolutely love their food and wine and want to be a part of food culture ... that's how the Festival shapes itself, that's how it grows. It's unstoppable. JILL DUPLEIX, 2010

Yet prior to the Melbourne Food and Wine Festival coming along to celebrate and highlight this food and wine culture, this aspect of the city was largely taken for granted except by a small circle of hardcore foodies.

But then several things happened to change that: the recession of the 1990s blew into town, Melbourne lost its bid to stage the 1996 Olympic Games and Peter Clemenger, chairman of the failed Olympic bid, took the holiday he'd promised his wife they'd take at the end of the bidding process. He began to think about what he could do to help rebuild and restore pride in the city.

Weighing up Melbourne's strengths he came to the conclusion that one of the things the city did best was events, and he "dreamt up" the plans for a food and wine festival. Back in Melbourne, Clemenger set about assembling a committee of people — restaurateur Richard Frank, wine expert Sarah Gough and food writer Jill Dupleix — to address the question of how to celebrate the city's great innate love of food in a way that didn't talk down to a population who were well-travelled, restaurant-savvy and aware of what was going on in the world of food.

An initial meeting in 1991 gave birth to a series of events that remain at the core of the Festival 20 years later. MasterClass, Restaurant Week (now Restaurant Express), the World's Longest Lunch, Winemaker Dinners and the Legends of Food and Wine were all put on the table early on.

Jill Dupleix, given the nod by Clemenger to run the Festival, realised she couldn't give the event the time it deserved and pulled back to a (still ongoing) advisory role, but not before recommending Sylvia Johnson, a restaurant owner who was known as "a good organiser with the ability to pull people together".

That hurdle cleared the way for the inevitable funding conundrum. Five months of work had gone into the planning of the Festival and, just like the Olympic bid, it seemed as if it wasn't going to get off the ground. That wasn't something that Clemenger was willing to swallow again and so he decided to finance the Festival himself — and would do so for the next nine years.

"People talk about the Melbourne Food and Wine Festival being a not-for-profit organisation," says Clemenger. "In my case I was looking at it in terms of being not-for-loss."

One of the great triumphs of that first Melbourne Food and Wine Festival was in creating a template that helped change the way Melbourne saw itself. It didn't reinvent the city, it just shone a spotlight on certain aspects and certain corners of the city.

In that first year the Festival held the World's Longest Lunch on a single table for 400 people at the Melbourne Cricket Ground, a dinner on stage at the Melbourne Concert Hall and breakfast at the Queen Victoria Market. At night the Queen Vic transformed into the colourful, lively, noisy Hawkers' Market. At the first MasterClass, hosted by the Grand Hyatt, the 32 presenters included Italian chef Giuliano Bugialli, who charmed the crowd with both his accent and pasta-making skills, and a roll call of home-grown talent like Stephanie Alexander, Greg Brown, Len Evans, Jonathan Gianfreda and Phillip Jones.

In a display of solidarity, the foodhalls of the city's three department stores — Myer, David Jones and Daimaru — banded together to offer a progressive feast; and over the years the skills of some of the state's top chefs — including Philippe Mouchel, Hermann Schneider, Greg Malouf and Alla Wolf-Tasker — were up for grabs in a "Win a Home Dinner Party" Competition.

This page from left: Jacob Freitag, Thorsten Schmidt, Adam D'Sylva, Darren Purchese, Jude Blereau, Harry Parr, Sam Bompas, Stephanie Alexander, Aphra Paine, Philippe Mouchel, Alexa Johnston, Rachel Allen, Roy Choi and Atul Kochhar, 2011.

Perhaps the most important event that first year, the one that added weight and soul and history (and perhaps even longevity) to the proceedings was the dinner honouring the Food and Wine Festival Legends, the leaders, groundbreakers and visionaries of the industry. The event was initially to be a one-off event, but it proved so popular and brought to light so many more people in the industry who deserved to be so honoured that the Legends immediately became an integral, ongoing part of the Festival's personality.

In the lead-up to the Festival's 10th birthday, Natalie O'Brien joined the team as CEO and soon after recruited food journalist (and now television personality) Matt Preston as Creative Director in 2005. Preston is a big man who brought huge energy to this role and an unconventional attitude towards working hours. He bombarded the Festival team with a constant flow of ideas that often arrived on the back of serviettes or beer coasters and were often overly ambitious (a plan to have waiters for the World's Longest Lunch by the Yarra River arrive in a submarine that would surface from the water and have them all spilling out to serve was one that hit the reject pile, as was another to hang a restaurant from a crane).

That same year there were two breakthroughs that saw the Festival attain a degree of financial security for the first time. Firstly, *The Age* newspaper came on board as a sponsor, which assured the Festival media support and enabled it to attract a wider range of sponsors because of that support. The second breakthrough was that

This page from left: Sally Wise, Alla Wolf-Tasker, Zakary Pelaccio, Elena Arzak, Geoff Lindsay, Margaret Xu, Rosa Mitchell, Martin Boetz, Andrew Blake, Ho Chi Ho, George Calombaris, Michael Bannerman, Jun Yukimura, Rob McLeary, Angela Hartnett, Anna Hansen, Greg Feck, Pedro Miguel Schiaffino, Toshiro Konishi, 2011.

the Festival worked collaboratively with Slow Food International, thus increasing its profile and the support from Victorian government.

The Melbourne Food and Wine Festival has deservedly elevated itself to iconic status. It attracts the biggest names on the planet who return to their respective countries and wax lyrical about Melbourne and Victoria which provides further momentum to this incredible event. ALASTAIR McLEOD, 2009

In 2006, Melbourne played host to the Commonwealth Games and, as they were held in March, the Melbourne Food and Wine Festival replaced its usual program with a more modest series of Rick Stein-led seafood events at Docklands in February. Though the Festival no-show seemed like a setback at first, it actually had a positive effect. The hiatus gave the Festival team time to take a breath and work on where to go next. It also made Melburnians realise how much they'd come to expect the Festival every March.

The Commonwealth Games also gave the Festival an opportunity to reach a wider crowd than just the hardcore food fans. At the live sites that had been set up for the Games around town, the Festival staged a series of events called the Culinary Pro-Am where teams of chefs representing various countries competed against each other to win the gold medal for cooking.

It was through the connections of some of the Festival's regular Australian contributors that it was able to attract some of the biggest international names to the Festival. Neil Perry was instrumental in bringing Heston Blumenthal and Thomas Keller to Melbourne for the 2007 Festival, while chef Raymond Capaldi played the friendship card with his mate Anthony Bourdain to get him to front the Festival, just as Bourdain's highly influential book *Kitchen Confidential* was beginning to make waves.

With the Festival also being asked to manage events like the visit by Spain's Ferran Adrià to promote his new book, it had achieved a certain robust momentum. Adrià's publishers were expecting a crowd of about 200 people but, in a display of Melbourne's food fanaticism, the chef and his interpreter played to a sold-out audience at the 1,500-seat State Theatre that could easily have sold out a second time.

Melbourne's Food and Wine scene is a fundamental part of what makes Melbourne unique. It draws on our ethnic diversity, excitement for new flavours and cultures and passion for life. SHANE DELIA, 2010

With Matt Preston finishing up as Creative Director in 2009, three major committees covering gastronomy, wine and umbrella events were introduced to create the themes and directions for the Festival's future.

The Festival has shone a spotlight on the diversity of Melbourne that has "engendered a great sense of community across the city",

says Tony Tan, an integral part of the event's creative team, tapping into both the city's intellectual side and its readiness for a bit of food-and-wine-inspired fun. That fun now spans two decades and encompasses a state, its capital city and the memories of hundreds of thousands of Festival-goers who have come together to eat and drink communally under the Melbourne Food and Wine Festival banner. It includes all the winemakers and chefs, bakers and producers, marketers and purveyors, and writers and teachers who have gathered with their colleagues and brethren from interstate and overseas in a place where the art of eating and drinking well can be discussed and participated in passionately, knowledgeably and with an understanding that it truly is one of life's great joys.

Peter Clemenger's idea, conceived to help a city lift itself from the doldrums, has exceeded his wildest expectations and has helped to engender a sense of confidence, purpose and place. It has shown Melbourne to be a city that leads, reflects and listens to what is happening in the world of food and wine because food and wine are part of its lifeblood. And with no shortage of tenacity and vision, the Melbourne Food and Wine Festival will continue to be a place where the world gathers to show how truly powerful the simple act of eating and drinking together can be.

Valerio Nucci, 2001.

George Calombaris, Langham
Melbourne MasterClass, 2011.

Chapter one

Local Legends

The Melbourne Food and Wine Festival has always been good at identifying and inviting great overseas chefs, but it's been just as good at gathering the best from a comfortably broad stock of home-grown talent. And it's interesting to note that many of the locals sell out their sessions as rapidly as any of the international stars. Stephanie Alexander and Maggie Beer, two long-time Festival friends, both writers of enormously influential cookbooks and proven masters of the MasterClass format, always book out quickly whenever they appear at the Festival but when, as they did in 2011, they appear together, the tickets are among the Festival's most sought after.

Above, from left to right: Margaret Fulton, 2003; Kylie Kwong and Stefano de Pieri, Delicious Double Acts, 2004; Stephanie Alexander and Maggie Beer, Delicious Double Acts, 2004; Curtis Stone and Shannon Bennett, Delicious Double Acts, 2004; Guy Grossi; Terry Durack and Jill Dupleix, Langham Melbourne MasterClass 2007.

Margaret Fulton

Presented in 2004

Gougères

Makes 30

The perfect accompaniment to a glass of wine, gougères are ideal for making ahead of time. Simply shape them on a baking tray and freeze. When they are frozen, transfer into freezer bags ready for baking any time.

150 g (5½ oz/1 cup) plain (all-purpose) flour

250 ml (9 fl oz/1 cup) milk

125 g (4½ oz) unsalted butter, cut into pieces

1 teaspoon sugar

½ teaspoon salt

4 eggs, lightly beaten, plus 1 extra if needed

150 g (5½ oz) Gruyère cheese, grated

beaten egg, for glazing

Preheat the oven to 220°C (425°F/Gas 7).

Sift the flour onto a square of baking paper.

Put the milk, butter, sugar and salt into a saucepan. Bring to a rapid boil and, using the baking paper as a funnel, pour the flour all at once into the boiling mixture. Over a gentle heat, incorporate quickly and thoroughly with a wooden spoon, beating until the mixture balls around the spoon and leaves the side of the pan (a bit of muscle is needed here). This process dries the paste and cooks the flour. Remove from the heat, transfer to a plate and cool to lukewarm.

Put into a bowl and gradually beat in the eggs. If the paste is very stiff, gradually beat in an extra egg until a pliable consistency is obtained. Beat the paste until well combined, shiny and smooth, then beat in the cheese using a wooden spoon.

Spoon small balls of the mixture on a buttered baking tray, brush with a little beaten egg and bake for 20 minutes or until puffed and golden. Serve piping hot.

Stephanie Alexander OAM

Snails on the grass

Serves 6–8

This combination of tiny soufflés and brilliant green sauce results in a rather fanciful dish that was very popular for many years at Stephanie's Restaurant. It was important to me as it enabled me to support one of our bravest specialist suppliers, Irena Votavova. Sadly there was not sufficient support for Irena and she had to discontinue snail farming. The recipe for the soufflés is very well known and the quantities given would make four conventional soufflés. In this dish, the mixture is baked in small porcelain demi-tasse cups, so that the finished soufflés are small and in scale with the puff pastry "snail shells".

Twice-cooked goat's cheese soufflés

Twice-cooked goat's cheese soufflés
80 g (2¾ oz) butter
60 g (2¼ oz) plain (all-purpose) flour
350 ml (12 fl oz) warm milk
75 g (2⅔ oz) fresh goat's cheese
1 tablespoon freshly grated parmesan
2 tablespoons freshly chopped parsley, or parsley and other herbs
3 egg yolks
4 egg whites
500 ml (17 fl oz/2 cups) pouring (single) cream

Preheat the oven to 180°C (350°F/Gas 4).

Melt 20 g (¾ oz) of the butter and grease 6–8 small demi-tasse cups or soufflé dishes. Melt the remaining butter in a small heavy-based saucepan. Stir in the flour and cook over medium heat, continuing to stir, for 2 minutes. Gradually add the milk, stirring all the while. Bring to boil, then reduce the heat and simmer for 5 minutes.

Mash the goat's cheese until soft and add to the hot sauce with the parmesan and parsley. Allow to cool for a few minutes. Fold the yolks in thoroughly and season with salt and freshly ground black pepper. Beat the egg white until creamy and fold quickly and lightly into the cheese mixture. Divide the mixture between the prepared moulds and smooth the surface of each. Stand the moulds in a baking dish lined with a tea towel and pour in boiling water to come two-thirds of the way up the sides of the moulds.

Bake for about 20 minutes or until firm to the touch and well puffed. Remove the soufflés from the oven — they will deflate and look wrinkled. Rest for a minute or so, then gently ease them out of their moulds. Invert onto a plate covered with plastic wrap and set aside.

"Snail shells"

puff pastry, cut into thin strips

Parsley and garlic cream sauce

5 garlic cloves, unpeeled

500 ml (17 fl oz/2 cups) pouring (single) cream

2 cups loosely-packed young parsley leaves, washed and dried

Snails

36–48 snails (ready cooked)

40 g (1½ oz) butter

2 garlic cloves, finely chopped

3 tablespoons roasted hazelnuts, chopped

2 teaspoons Pernod

To serve

baby salad leaves

To serve, place the soufflés upside down in a buttered ovenproof gratin dish, so that they are not touching. Pour over the cream (60 ml (2 fl oz/¼ cup) per soufflé) to moisten them thoroughly. Return to the oven for 15 minutes. The soufflés will look swollen and golden.

"Snail shells"

Increase the oven to 200°C (400°F/Gas 6). Create puff pastry snail shells by winding a thin strip of puff pastry around a lightly oiled ovenproof mould (such as sake cups). Bake the shells for 10–15 minutes or until well browned. Allow to cool a little before slipping the shells from the moulds.

Parsley and garlic cream sauce

Place the unpeeled garlic in a small saucepan and cover with cold water. Bring slowly to the boil, then pour off the water. Repeat this twice more to rid the garlic of any bitterness. Slip the garlic cloves from their skins. Bring the garlic and cream slowly to simmering point in the rinsed-out pan. Remove the pan from the heat. Check the garlic is quite soft — if not, simmer in the cream a further 5 minutes. Add the parsley to the hot cream and immediately blend in a blender, a small quantity at a time, to a smooth green sauce. Season with salt and white pepper. The sauce can be used at once, stored or reheated. Makes 2½ cups.

Snails

When the soufflés and sauce are made, melt the butter in a large frying pan and sauté the snails with the garlic, hazelnuts and Pernod until hot.

To serve

Spread 2–3 tablespoons of sauce on each plate to represent the grass. Arrange 2 small "bushes" of the salad leaves at each end of the grass. Tumble the hot snails near to the bushes and top with the "snail shells".

From *Stephanie's Australia: Travelling and Tasting*, Stephanie Alexander, Allen & Unwin Pty Ltd (1991).

Hermann Schneider

Presented in 1998

Aged lamb rump with chermoula poached in reduced stock flavoured with sherry

Serves 4

4 aged whole lamb rumps

4 lamb neck bones

1 carrot, chopped

1 large onion, chopped

2 sticks celery, chopped

1 sprig thyme

1 sprig marjoram

1 fresh bay leaf

1 bunch baby turnips

12 shallots or tiny salad onions

1 bunch baby Dutch carrots

1 tablespoon ghee or clarified butter

50 g (1¾ oz) unsalted butter

1 cup baby broad (fava) beans (skins removed) or fresh peas

150 ml (5 fl oz) medium-dry sherry

1 tablespoon chopped mixed coriander (cilantro), parsley and chives

continued >

Have the butcher bone out the rumps and keep the fillet ends and trimmings for another dish. Remove all the fat from the rumps. Set the rumps aside.

Place the neck bones in a large saucepan, cover with cold water and bring to the boil. Drain, then return to the pan. Add the carrot, onion, celery, thyme, marjoram and bay leaf, then pour in enough cold water to cover. Bring to the boil over high heat, then reduce the heat to low and simmer for 2 hours, skimming often. Strain, then return the stock to a clean pan and simmer over medium heat until syrupy and reduced to 300–350 ml (10½–12 fl oz). Discard the solids.

Meanwhile, to make the chermoula, place all the ingredients, except the olive oil, in a blender. With the motor running, gradually add the oil until puréed.

Clean the turnips, shallots and baby carrots carefully, leaving 5 mm (¼ inch) of green on all the vegetable tops.

Heat the ghee in a large heavy-based frying pan over medium–high heat. Brown the rumps on both sides, then remove from the pan and place on a wire rack to cool.

Spread each lamb rump with a generous amount of chermoula, then place each rump into individual freezer bags and tie securely. Place in a saucepan of water heated to 70°C (150°F) and cook for 15 minutes, then remove to a warm place to rest.

Chermoula

1 medium onion, finely chopped

4 tablespoons flat-leaf (Italian)
parsley, chopped

¼ teaspoon saffron powder

¼ teaspoon mixed paprika and
cayenne

2 tablespoons lemon juice

1 garlic clove

4 tablespoons coriander (cilantro)
leaves, chopped

1 teaspoon ground cumin

125 ml (4 fl oz/½ cup) olive oil

In a large frying pan, glaze the shallots in 25 g (1 oz) of the butter. After a few minutes, add the turnips and carrots, wet with a little reduced stock and gently cook for a few minutes or until *al dente*, adding the broad beans or peas in the final moments.

To serve, place the remaining reduced lamb stock and the sherry in a small saucepan and bring to a gentle simmer. Slice the pink rumps, arrange on a plate, adding any lamb juices to the stock. Garnish the plates with the jardinière of glazed vegetables, then whisk the remaining 25 g (1 oz) of the butter into the sauce, add the herbs and adjust the seasoning. Generously coat the meat with the sauce and serve immediately.

My favourite thing about Melbourne Food and Wine Festival is meeting new people, sharing ideas, making new friends, cooking for people who understand and appreciate your work. BEN SHEWRY, 2009

Presented in 2009

Verjuice custard with bergamot-braised raisin clusters

Serves 6

Preheat the oven to 120°C (235°F/Gas ½).

For the verjuice custard, heat the cream with the rosemary sprig to just before scalding.

Place the verjuice in a small saucepan and simmer over low heat until reduced to 200 ml (7 fl oz).

Whisk the whole egg, egg yolk and sugar until combined but do not overwhisk and allow too much air into the mixture or it will go "foamy" when the verjuice is added.

Whisking continuously, add the hot verjuice slowly in a thin stream to the egg mixture, then add the hot cream in the same way. Strain through a fine-mesh sieve, skim any foam from the top and pour into six 125 ml (4 fl oz/½ cup) capacity moulds.

Place in a water bath (see Notes), cover with foil and bake for 50–60 minutes or until softly set. Leave to cool overnight in the fridge to firmly set. They may melt if taken out of the fridge too long in advance.

Notes: I use Bulla thickened cream.

Line the bottom of the water bath with a tea towel to stop excessive radiant heat that will result in a "ring" of a different consistency on the tops of the custards.

This recipe can be increased by four times before you need to be concerned about the egg-to-verjuice ratio.

Verjuice custard

350 ml (12 fl oz) cream (40% fat) *(see Notes)*

1 sprig rosemary

375 ml (13 fl oz/1½ cups) verjuice

110 g (3¾ oz) whole egg

100 g (3½ oz) egg yolk

100 g (3½ oz) caster (superfine) sugar

continued >

Maggie Beer, Hands-On
MasterClass, 2011.

Bergamot-braised raisin clusters

125 g (4½ oz) raisin (muscatel) clusters on stems

60 g (2¼ oz) caster (superfine) sugar

185 ml (6 fl oz/¾ cup) verjuice

1 g Earl Grey tea leaves

30 ml (1 fl oz) boiling water, plus extra for soaking raisins

Verjuice and tea infused syrup

2 g Earl Grey tea leaves

50 ml (1¾ fl oz) boiling water

35 g (1¼ oz) caster (superfine) sugar

100 ml (3½ fl oz) verjuice

For the bergamot-braised raisin clusters, place the raisins in a heatproof bowl, cover with boiling water and stand for 45 minutes.

Place the sugar and verjuice in a small saucepan and stir over low heat until the sugar dissolves. Bring to the boil, then simmer until reduced by one-third.

Infuse the tea in the boiling water for 5 minutes, then strain and add to the sugar syrup.

Drain the raisins from the soaking water and add to the sugar syrup mixture. Place back on the heat and allow to coat the raisins without reducing the syrup too much as the raisins will crystallise on cooling.

For the verjuice and tea infused syrup, combine the tea and boiling water and allow to infuse for 4–5 minutes. Strain.

Combine the sugar, verjuice and tea liquid in a saucepan and bring to the boil over medium heat. Reduce the heat to low and simmer for 8–10 minutes or until reduced by approximately half, then set aside to cool.

To serve

Dip the bases of the custards briefly in hot water, then invert onto plates. Serve with a sprig of the braised raisin clusters and a little verjuice and tea infused syrup.

Making Legends

Conceived as a one-off event for the first Festival in 1993, the naming of each year's Melbourne Food and Wine Festival Legends has since become something of a touchstone event. Some would even argue it's what gives the Festival its soul. By acknowledging and honouring the people who helped build Melbourne's wine and food culture, the Festival links the past with the way that we will eat and drink in the future. It shows respect for those who have done the groundwork, who have helped make Melbourne "Melbourne". It also shows that, in a city that takes its food and wine seriously, there's always room for another celebration.

Strict ground rules about who can gain Legend status were laid down from the very beginning. The award for the quite sizeable initial crop (the large number due to the event being conceived as a one-off and the original committee not wanting to miss anybody) was created to pay tribute to "the leaders, groundbreakers and visionaries of Victoria's food and wine industry". It wasn't enough to be running a successful business — there were other kinds of awards for that. Legends were chosen because they "are driven by a passion to strive for groundbreaking perfection … they inspire and inform the public, the media and their peers, enriching Victoria's food and wine culture". That there are now more than 100 Legends in the Hall of Fame, gives some idea of how committed to (or perhaps fanatical about) the art of eating and drinking many Victorians are.

There were three original categories by which people could have Legend status bestowed: Food Production and Education, Grape Growing or Winemaking, and the Hospitality Industry. In 2007 a further category was added for Interstate or International Legends. This was to be awarded to Victorians who had made a major contribution to developing food and wine cultures interstate or overseas or to people from outside of the state who had had significant influence on Victoria's food and wine culture

through their presence, their impact through the media or on the chefs, winemakers and producers they've inspired. These recipients have included Rose Gray, Antonio Carluccio, Michel Roux, Damien Pignolet, Cheong Liew and Tony Bilson.

The first Legends were honoured at a dinner at Queens Hall in Parliament House. Pamela Bakes, one of the Festival's original paid employees, who helped to organise the dinner and choose the initial recipients, feels that it was something of a defining moment for the Melbourne Food and Wine Festival.

"Even though the food was dreadful — some sort of duck that was so tough you could barely chew it — it was very exciting to see all the old guard of the Melbourne food scene in the one room at the one time. It was the first time that it was formally recognised that Victoria had some kind of food and wine scene that was so much part of the culture of the city. These people had really made Melbourne what it was in terms of food so that the dinner was absolutely wonderful, a huge success."

Among the recipients of that first batch were giants and founders of the Victorian wine industry, people like Doug Crittenden, Norman Killeen, Mick Morris, John Brown and Alan Watson, the owner of one of Melbourne's original small bars. Also included were many members of city's famed "spaghetti mafia", the Italian restaurateurs like Leon Massoni, Joe Molina, Mario Virgona and Rino Codognotto, who had defined a particular kind of generous, sophisticated dining experience in Melbourne. Also honoured were Gilbert Lau, who had helped put Melbourne on the dining map with his superb Cantonese restaurant, Flower Drum; Vincent Rosales, the man behind Maxim's, one of Melbourne's first true fine-dining establishments; and Elizabeth Chong, one of the city's great food educators.

After 1993, the number of Legends named every year was usually limited to around five with the roll call including a range of farmers, winemakers, restaurateurs, writers, journalists, educators, cafe owners, cheesemakers and caterers.

Initially, it was the members of the Food and Wine Festival committee who were responsible for putting forward likely candidates, but in time, there were enough names in the Hall of Fame for the nominating process to be handed over to them. Those who have been honoured are now the ones doing the honouring. The cycle of respect and acknowledgement is firmly established and Melbourne is a better place for it.

Clockwise from top left: Stephanie Alexander (photographed by Simon Schluter, courtesy of *The Age*); Leo Pellegrini (photograph courtesy of *The Age*); Jonathon Gianfreda (photograph courtesy of *The Age*); Geoff Dobson (photographed by Simon Schluter, courtesy of *The Age*); Mietta O'Donnell (photograph courtesy of *The Age*); James Halliday.

Damien Pignolet

Presented in 1997

Rabbit rillettes

(Rillettes de lapin)

Serves 6–8

To make the quatre-épices, the best results will be achieved using whole spices that are ground in a blender or coffee grinder (that is kept solely for spice grinding). Combine the ground spices and seal in a jar.

Preheat the oven to 150°C (300°F/Gas 2).

Portion the rabbit into legs, forelegs and cut the loin into 4 pieces. Cut the pork belly and back fat into 5 cm (2 inch) cubes. Place all the meat, back fat, lard and water in a deep frying pan, preferably so that there are no more than 2 layers (i.e. rabbit-leg depth).

Cover, place in the oven and cook until the meats and fat are all very soft, possibly up to 1¾–2 hours. Check the temperature to see that it does not roast or fry.

Remove from the oven, take out the rabbit pieces and deal with it first. Scald a bowl with boiling water and dry it with a clean cloth. Carefully remove the meat from the bones. Place the meat in the bowl and, using two forks, tear into strips.

Then do the same with the pork and combine with the rabbit.

Mix a sufficient amount of the cooking fat to bind the rillettes, adding salt, pepper and quatre-épices to taste. (You might like to add a little spirit such as Armagnac, about 2–3 teaspoons.) Pack very tightly into sterilised jars, knocking down the contents frequently to remove air pockets. Clean the jars of anything that is smeared around the rim. Melt some fresh lard, allow to cool, then pour into the jars to a depth of 5 cm (2 inches) to seal the rillettes. When the lard is set, seal with baking paper and foil and mark with the name of the contents and the production date. Enjoy with crusty bread.

2 rabbits (1–1.2 kg/
2 lb 4 oz–2 lb 10 oz each)

400 g (14 oz) piece fat pork belly, skinned

150 g (5½ oz) pork back fat

100 g (3½ oz) lard, plus extra for sealing

50 ml (1¾ fl oz) water

salt and pepper

quatre-épices *(see recipe below)*

crusty bread, to serve

Quatre-épices

3½ teaspoons ground allspice

½ teaspoon ground nutmeg

½ teaspoon ground cloves

½ teaspoon ground cinnamon

Damien Pignolet, Langham
Melbourne MasterClass, 2008.

Presented in 1999

Braised lamb neck with barley pilaf

Serves 12

Stuffing

2 onions, chopped

100 g (3½ oz) unsalted butter

1 teaspoon freshly ground black pepper

1 teaspoon ground ginger

1 teaspoon cumin seeds, toasted and crushed

120 g (4¼ oz/2 cups) fresh breadcrumbs

1 teaspoon salt

1 teaspoon toasted and crushed coriander seeds

140 g (5 oz) toasted pistachio nuts

2 eggs

Lamb

12 × 600 g (1 lb 5 oz) lamb necks, deboned (yielding about 300 g/10½ oz meat)

500 g (1 lb 2 oz) caul fat

12 pieces muslin (cheesecloth) (20 cm × 20 cm/8 × 8 inches)

kitchen string

olive oil, for cooking

continued >

Preheat the oven to 175°C (345°F/Gas 3–4).

To make the stuffing, cook the onion in butter until golden, then combine with the remaining stuffing ingredients and cool.

To assemble the lamb, cut the neck meat in half lengthways and discard the "paddywhack". Add the stuffing and wrap in caul fat, then tie in muslin. Heat the olive oil in a large heavy-based ovenproof saucepan and brown the necks.

Braise

olive oil, for cooking

1 onion, chopped

1 carrot, chopped

½ stick celery, chopped

1 tablespoon black peppercorns

1 litre (35 fl oz/4 cups) lamb stock
(or chicken stock)

rind of 1 lemon, removed in strips

1 teaspoon coriander seeds,
toasted

1 tablespoon salt

1 teaspoon saffron threads

20 garlic cloves

1 teaspoon ground ginger

1 teaspoon cumin seeds, toasted

Barley pilaf

1 large onion, finely chopped

125 g (4½ oz) unsalted butter

225 g (8 oz) pearl barley

½ cup dried barberries (optional)

1 litre (35 fl oz/4 cups) water

½ teaspoon toasted cumin seeds

2 teaspoons salt

1 teaspoon freshly ground black or
white pepper

140 g (5 oz/1 cup) currants

2 tablespoons lemon juice

finely grated zest of 2 lemons

To braise the necks, heat a little olive oil in a frying pan. Brown the onion, carrot and celery, then add these to the necks. Add the remaining braising ingredients to the necks. Bring to the boil, seal the pan with foil and braise in the oven for 1–2 hours.

When cool, carefully take off the muslin and degrease the braising liquid very well. Strain the braising liquid, pressing the garlic cloves through the sieve to thicken the sauce.

To make the barley pilaf, reduce the oven to 150°C (300°F/Gas 2). In a heavy-based ovenproof saucepan, cook the onion in the butter until golden. Add the barley and barberries and brown further. Add the remaining ingredients, except the lemon juice and zest. Seal with foil and cook in the oven for 1 hour. Add the lemon juice and zest and check the seasoning.

To serve, cut the lamb necks into thirds and serve with the barley pilaf and sauce.

Foodie Films,
Federation Square, 2010.

Alla Wolf-Tasker AM

Presented in 2009

Smoked eel brandade with cucumber

Serves 4–6

Brandade croquettes

about 800 g (1 lb 12 oz) cleaned and deboned smoked eel fillet

3–4 confit garlic cloves (optional)

1 kg (2 lb 4 oz) boiled potatoes, peeled then passed through a mouli and kept warm

about 150 ml (5 fl oz) extra virgin olive oil, warmed (quantity depends on the fattiness of the eel)

100 ml (3½ fl oz) milk (warm)

freshly ground white pepper

4 large eggs

300 g (10½ oz/2 cups) plain (all-purpose) flour

300 g (10½ oz) breadcrumbs (preferably panko)

vegetable oil, for deep-frying

To make the brandade croquettes, preheat the oven to 170°C (325°F/Gas 3).

Cut the eel fillet into pieces and pulse in a food processor with the confit garlic, if using, until a coarse purée. Scrape into a large bowl and add the warm potato, olive oil, milk and pepper. Beat together with a wooden spoon or with an electric beater until the mixture just comes together. Taste and adjust the seasoning.

Divide the mixture into 12 portions and roll into croquettes. Alternatively, shape into quenelles with large spoons. Chill the shaped portions or even place in the freezer for a few minutes to make crumbing easier.

Whisk the eggs in a bowl. Dust each croquette lightly in the flour, dip in the whisked egg and coat with the breadcrumbs.

Heat the oil to 180°C (350°F). Fry the croquettes just until golden brown. Drain on paper towel.

Place on a baking tray to finish cooking in the oven, about 6 minutes. If you are not serving until later, reduce the oven heat to low.

Cucumber salad

3 medium cucumbers

salt and pepper

lemon and olive oil dressing (1 part lemon juice to 3 parts extra virgin olive oil, mixed with salt and pepper)

fresh dill, finely chopped

Herbed crème fraîche

300 g (10½ oz) crème fraîche

6 chives, finely chopped

3 sprigs dill, finely chopped

To make the cucumber salad, peel and deseed the cucumbers. Using a swivel peeler, cut ribbons down the length of the cucumbers and all around. Cut the ribbons into fine julienne. Sprinkle the cucumber with a little salt and leave to drain in a colander for 10 minutes. Quickly rinse the cucumber under running water and dry. Toss with the dressing. Add the chopped dill to taste and season with salt and pepper.

To make the herbed crème fraîche, combine the ingredients in a bowl.

Serve the brandade croquettes with the cucumber salad and herbed crème fraîche.

Frankly I've never seen a festival so genuinely embraced by such a diverse audience. Food has the capacity to engage and link people, and the Melbourne Food and Wine Festival delivers that sense of engagement in spades. From high-end haute cuisine to local events in small rural communities, there's a real buzz. ALLA WOLF-TASKER, 2009

Cheong Liew

Presented in 2007

Braised spiced pork belly with smoked whole garlic

Serves 6–8

1 kg (2 lb 4 oz) piece boneless
pork belly

rice bran oil, for pan-frying

500 ml (17 fl oz/2 cups) water

6 large dried chillies

2 whole bulbs smoked garlic
(see Note)

20 g (¾ oz) rock sugar, crushed

Marinade

60 ml (2 fl oz/¼ cup) light soy
sauce

2 tablespoons sugar

2 tablespoons dark soy sauce

2 tablespoons white rice wine

½ teaspoon salt

1 star anise

2 cinnamon sticks

20 g (¾ oz) sliced ginger

Cut the pork belly into 2 cm (¾ inch) pieces, mix well with the marinade, then cover and refrigerate overnight or at least 6 hours.

Drain the pork, reserving the marinade and pat dry on paper towel. In a deep saucepan, heat a little oil and fry the marinated pork until lightly brown. Add the water, left-over marinade, chillies, whole garlic and rock sugar. Bring to the boil and simmer until tender and the cooking liquid thickens. Serve with yellow spiced rice.

Note: To make smoked garlic, soak the whole bulbs in warm water for 20 minutes, then roast on a naked flame (as if you are roasting capsicum/pepper or eggplant/aubergine). Remove the burnt black skin, then it is ready to use.

World's Longest Lunch

Just like MasterClass, the World's Longest Lunch is one of the Melbourne Food and Wine Festival's most endearing and enduring events. It's also something of a signature, able to encapsulate in a beautifully dressed, 400 metre-long table packed with revellers in some of Melbourne's most iconic locations what the heart of the Festival is all about — a mass celebration of the joys of eating and drinking well. It's also one of the most loved events in the program and has now spread from the city into regional Victoria with more than 25 separate lunches being held simultaneously across the state in botanic gardens, on bridges and in wineries.

The fate and the size of the Longest Lunch table have, over the years, provided something of a mirror to the fortunes and popularity of the Festival as a whole. In 1993, for example, when the Festival was in its inaugural year, the Melbourne Cricket Ground, one of the world's great sporting arenas, was the chosen location for the World's Longest Lunch, a statement-making move by a new event wanting to announce that it had arrived. But as the day of the first Longest Lunch approached, many seats on the 400-seat table were unsold, so Festival Chairman Peter Clemenger subsidised tickets for about 75 of his advertising company staff to fill the empty spaces. The event was a success, word of mouth spread and neither Clemenger nor anybody else has had to put their hand in their pocket to salvage the event again.

Every year now when the Festival announces its line-up of events, the location of World's Longest Lunch is one of the most anticipated pieces of information and space at the table is eagerly sought after. Over the years, the Longest Lunch has seen the table grow from the original 400 seats to over 1,000. The logistics of staging an event such as this, most often

World's Longest Lunch, Carlton Gardens, 2011.

in untried locations, are mind-boggling, with caterers having to bring in generators, portable kitchens, fleets of staff and tonnes of food, not to mention the careful setting of a table that seats 1,000 people and bathroom facilities to cater to the sizeable crowd.

In 1999 the location for the World's Longest Lunch was to be at New Quay Promenade, on the water in Docklands, but a forecast of inclement weather had forced a rethink of the location and so the table (and the kitchens, generators and everything else involved with World's Longest Lunch) was moved inside to one of the huge old storage sheds nearby. On the day of the lunch, however, the weather turned fine and (then) Festival Director Sylvia Johnson made the last-minute decision to move the whole lot outside again, saying that there "would have been a riot if we'd made people eat inside those dusty old sheds on such a beautiful day".

One of the greatest feats of outside catering came with the 2005 event staged in the forecourt of Melbourne Museum, which was a collaboration between Gilbert Lau and Anthony Lui, from the Flower Drum, and Tony Le Deux, an independent caterer who was a driving force behind six of the Festival's Longest Lunches. Not only was Le Deux allowed the rare privilege of working in the Flower Drum kitchen but he was part of perhaps the most ambitious menu the Longest Lunch had ever attempted: san choi bao, duck with wilted greens and ginger ice cream pyramids with Chinese glass jelly.

"To attempt a menu which required 1,000 crisp lettuce leaves and 1,000 servings of ice cream at an outside venue during the height of summer was madness," says Le Deux. "But the day ran like clockwork, the entertainment was spectacular, the service efficient and Gilbert Lau remarked it was the best Chinese banquet he has had outside the Flower Drum."

But with the World's Longest Lunch, the panic backstage is rarely communicated to those sitting at the table. They are more likely to remember being served fish and chips by street-smart young kids on rollerblades on St Kilda Pier or the sight of a ballerina getting up onto the table set on St Kilda Road outside the National Gallery and the Arts Centre and walking the entire 400 metre length of it as people were eating without dislodging a single glass, napkin, plate or fork. Or they might remember when Jamie Oliver lent his support to the Marysville Longest Lunch by appearing at the event the year after the town had been devastated by the Black Saturday bushfires.

Those moments, the theatricality of such en masse dining and the feeling of camaraderie have made World's Longest Lunch the highlight of the Festival for many people, something that shows no sign of fading as the grand event enters its third decade.

Clockwise from top left: World's Longest Lunch, Telstra Dome, 2007; World's Longest Lunch, Flemington Racecourse, 2008; World's Longest Lunch, Marysville, 2009; World's Longest Lunch, Fawkner Park, 2001; World's Longest Lunch, Docklands, 1995.

Tony Bilson

Presented in 1996

Fillet of beef roasted in red wine shallot bread

Serves 8

1 fillet of beef (about 1.5 kg/
3 lb 5 oz), fully trimmed and tied
with the tail folded to make
the fillet evenly shaped

Maldon sea salt, for sprinkling

6 sprigs thyme

4 fresh bay leaves

Marinade

1 tablespoon Dijon mustard

1 teaspoon freshly ground black
pepper

1 teaspoon chopped thyme

2 tablespoons olive oil

3 garlic cloves, crushed

1 tablespoon red wine vinegar

2 crushed fresh bay leaves

Red wine shallot bread

125 g (4½ oz) sliced shallots

500 ml (17 fl oz/2 cups)
young cabernet wine

1 fresh bay leaf

2 sprigs thyme

1 teaspoon black peppercorns

625 g (1 lb 6 oz) strong (baker's) flour

62.5 g (2¼ oz) fresh baker's yeast

1 teaspoon salt

Combine all the marinade ingredients. Brush the beef with the marinade mixture and refrigerate overnight or at least 2 hours.

Cook the fillet on a grill or in a preheated 250°C (500°F/Gas 9) oven until rare, then cool as quickly as possible.

To make the red wine shallot bread, boil the shallot, wine, bay leaf, thyme and peppercorns over high heat until reduced by half.

Place the flour, yeast, salt and shallot mixture (with the bay leaf and thyme sprigs removed first) in the bowl of an electric mixer fitted with a dough hook and knead on speed 2 for 15 minutes.

Roll out the dough into a rectangle large enough to envelop the beef fillet. Have the fillet at room temperature, with the string removed. Roll the dough around the fillet, seal the ends, brush with water and sprinkle with the Maldon sea salt, sprigs of thyme and bay leaves. Leave to rise at least 30 minutes.

Preheat the oven to 210°C (425°F/Gas 6–7). Bake the bread-wrapped beef fillet for 25 minutes. Remove from the oven, rest and cut into 3–4 cm (1¼–1½ inch) thick slices. Serve with baby green beans tossed in butter and baby carrots. As the beef is rare, it does not need a sauce but it may be wise to have some sauce Bordelaise on hand.

Maggie Beer

Presented in 2009

Warm salad of roasted pheasant with walnuts, citrus and bitter leaves

Serves 4

Pheasant

1 × 900 g (2 lb) whole pheasant

extra virgin olive oil

60 ml (2 fl oz/¼ cup) verjuice

Marinade

2 oranges, skin removed in wide strips and flesh juiced

6 sprigs thyme

4 fresh bay leaves

2 teaspoons crushed juniper berries

60 ml (2 fl oz/¼ cup) extra virgin olive oil

Pheasant jus

1 large onion, unpeeled, roughly chopped

2 small carrots, roughly chopped

2 sticks celery without leaves, roughly chopped

extra virgin olive oil, for drizzling

2 tablespoons verjuice

250 ml (9 fl oz/1 cup) golden chicken stock

French the wings of the pheasant. Remove any blood from inside the bird. Cut the legs away from the breast frame, keeping the legs as one piece. Cut away the backbone from the breast frame.

Combine the marinade ingredients in a bowl. Brush the entire skin of the pheasant pieces with the marinade, then leave, skin side down, in the marinade for 2 hours in the refrigerator.

Preheat the oven to 220°C (425°F/Gas 7). Place the breast sitting upright, skin side up, and the legs skin side up in a roasting tray and scatter with the bay leaves and orange strips from the marinade. Brush liberally with the extra virgin olive oil, sprinkle with sea salt and roast for 10 minutes to caramelise. Turn the temperature down to 200°C (400°F/Gas 6).

Turn the pheasant pieces over and after another 4 minutes (approximately), the legs will be ready to take out — put aside on a resting tray with the orange strips, bay leaves and juices from the roasting tray so they don't burn. Splash the legs with a little verjuice.

Return the tray to the oven to finish cooking the breast pieces — this could be another 4 minutes but feel to check.

Remove the tray from the oven and transfer the contents and the juices to the resting tray. Drizzle with the verjuice and turn the breasts, skin side down. Cover loosely with foil and rest for 20 minutes.

Allow to cool totally before carving using a very sharp knife. Cut each breast off the "cage" and put the cut side straight down into the juices of the resting tray. Reserve the carcass.

Vinaigrette

extra virgin olive oil

pheasant jus

vincotto

sea salt and freshly ground black
pepper

To finish

8 thin slices Black Pig belly bacon

butter, for cooking

4 chicken livers

40 g (1½ oz/⅓ cup) walnuts,
roasted and skins rubbed off

To assemble

1 small radicchio

1 large bulb white witlof
(chicory/ Belgian endive)

1 small bunch rocket (arugula)

1 baby fennel, thinly sliced
on a mandoline and drizzled
immediately with a sprinkle
of verjuice and extra virgin
olive oil, fronds reserved

3 tablespoons flat-leaf (Italian)
parsley leaves

Cut the drumstick off each of the legs and use to make the pheasant jus (because of the very sharp sinews) and then carefully take out the thigh bone from the centre of the thigh, making sure you take the piece of cartilage from the joint as well without cutting through the skin to keep the thigh intact. Place the cut side down in the juices that have accumulated until required.

For some pheasants, there will be enough natural jus on the resting plate, however, to utilise the bones to make a pheasant jus, chop the carcass and set aside with the drumsticks. Place the onion, carrot and celery in a flameproof roasting tray with a drizzle of olive oil and roast at 200°C (400°F/Gas 6) for 20 minutes or until caramelised. Place the tray on the stovetop over high heat and deglaze the tray with the verjuice, stirring well. Add the chopped carcass, drumsticks and chicken stock, then boil rapidly to reduce the sauce to a coating consistency. Strain and discard the solids. Set aside to use to add to the vinaigrette.

To make the vinaigrette, allow 2–3 tablespoons vinaigrette per serve. Combine a ratio of 3 parts olive oil to 2 parts pheasant jus and 1 part vincotto and season to taste.

To finish, in a dry non-stick frying pan, cook the belly bacon till well coloured on both sides. Place on a piece of paper towel briefly to drain, then add to the resting tray with the pheasant pieces.

Using another piece of paper towel, wipe out the pan and add a little butter till sizzling. Season and pan-fry the chicken livers over medium–high heat till just cooked and still pink inside. Add to the resting tray along with the roasted walnuts.

To assemble, put the resting tray into a 200°C (400°F/Gas 6) oven for about 2 minutes to warm through the contents. Quickly carve each breast in half, then carve each half into 3 slices on the diagonal. Slice each leg lengthways into 3 pieces.

Position the radicchio leaves, witlof and rocket on 4 individual plates.

In a large bowl, toss the pheasant pieces, bacon, livers, orange rind, fennel slices and reserved fronds, parsley and walnuts. Divide equally between the 4 plates, arranging on top of the leaves and drizzle with the vinaigrette. Finish with some sea salt and freshly ground black pepper.

Stefano de Pieri

Presented in 2002

Stracotto of lamb with olives and orange

Serves 4-6

Stracotto translates to "overcooked" in English. This melting dish is delicious for a cold winter night, when the delicate combination of olives and orange adds warming depth of flavour to the tangy gaminess of not-so-young lamb. Serve with cubes of sautéed pumpkin.

1 boneless leg of lamb (about 2.25 kg/5 lb), butterflied

salt and pepper

60 ml (2 fl oz/¼ cup) extra virgin olive oil

2 medium red onions, chopped into 1 cm (½ inch) dice

4 garlic cloves, peeled and left whole

2 anchovy fillets, rinsed and dried

2 oranges, quartered, deseeded, and sliced into 5-6 mm (¼ inch) quarter-moons

1 cup Tuscan green olives or picholines

125 ml (4 fl oz/½ cup) freshly squeezed orange juice

250 ml (9 fl oz/1 cup) Chianti or other dry red wine

250 ml (9 fl oz/1 cup) basic tomato sauce (sugo)

Preheat the oven to 170°C (325°F/Gas 3).

Trim most of the fat from the lamb and season to taste with the salt and pepper. In a large, heavy-based casserole, heat the oil until almost smoking. Brown the lamb on both sides until dark golden brown and remove to a side dish.

Add the onion, garlic, anchovies and orange pieces to the casserole and cook over medium heat until softened, 4-6 minutes, scraping the casserole base with a wooden spoon to loosen the brown bits.

Add the olives, orange juice, wine and tomato sauce and bring to the boil. Return the lamb to the casserole, bring to the boil, then cover and bake for 1½-2 hours or until fork-tender. Remove from the oven, then simmer over medium heat for 10-15 minutes or until the sauce has thickened and reduced. Slice the lamb and serve with the sauce.

Michel Roux, Langham
Melbourne MasterClass, 2008.

Chapter two

Around the World

Every year as the Melbourne Food and Wine Festival draws near there's the inevitable mounting excitement about which chefs from overseas will be touching down in Melbourne for the duration. This, afterall, is an event that has pulled together a head-spinningly impressive line-up of overseas talent. Equally impressive though is the number of cuisines from all around the world that have been featured in the Festival over the years, a reflection perhaps of the multicultural city — and country — in which it's based. This is particularly emphasised by the number of home-grown and Australian-based chefs who have, alongside their overseas counterparts, brought many different cuisines to the stage of MasterClass. Sydneysider Neil Perry has a love for Asian flavours but he's also a dab hand with those from the Middle East, while George Calombaris (and his mum) have treated audiences to a unique take on Greek and Cypriot cooking and Greg Malouf, the father of Modern Middle Eastern cooking in Australia, has opened people's eyes to the delights of sumac and orange blossom. Every year the Festival will feature flavours from nearly every continent, creating a three-week flavour trip around the world.

From left to right: Angela Hartnett, 2011; Fergus Henderson, 2008; Heston Blumenthal, 2009; Elena Arzak, 2011; Roy Choi, 2011; Massimo Bottura, 2010; Thierry Marx, 2007.

George Calombaris

Presented in 2011

Lamb koupes

Makes 20

To make the dough, place the burghul and 375 ml (13 fl oz/1½ cups) of boiling water in a heatproof bowl and soak for 2 hours. Process the soaked burghul, flour, ½ teaspoon salt and 60 ml (2 fl oz/¼ cup) of water in a food processor for 30 seconds or until the mixture forms a coarse-textured dough. Transfer to a bowl, cover, then rest for 15 minutes.

Meanwhile, to make the filling, heat the olive oil in a frying pan over high heat. Add the mince, breaking up with a wooden spoon, then cook, stirring occasionally, for 5 minutes or until starting to brown. Reduce the heat to low, add the onion and cook for 8 minutes or until the onion is soft. Stir in the cinnamon, almonds and parsley. Season with salt and pepper. Cool.

To make the koupes, using oiled hands, place 2 tablespoons of the dough in the palm of your hand and flatten to form an oval-shaped cup. Place 1 tablespoon of the filling in the centre, then bring up the sides of the dough to enclose. Seal the edges, then roll to form an oval shape. Repeat to make 20 koupes.

Fill a deep-fryer or large saucepan one-third full with vegetable oil. Heat to 180°C (350°F). Working in 4 batches, fry the koupes for 4 minutes or until golden. Remove with a slotted spoon and drain on paper towel. Season koupes with salt and serve immediately with lemon wedges.

320 g (11¼ oz) medium burghul (bulgur)

75 g (2⅔ oz/½ cup) plain (all-purpose) flour

2 tablespoons olive oil

250 g (9 oz) minced (ground) lamb

1 onion, finely chopped

½ teaspoon ground cinnamon

80 g (2¾ oz/½ cup) blanched almonds, roasted and finely chopped

½ cup flat-leaf (Italian) parsley, finely chopped

vegetable oil, for deep-frying

lemon wedges, to serve

Greg Malouf

Presented in 2000

Chicken and pistachio dolmades

Makes 20

250 g (9 oz) vine leaves

100 g (3½ oz/½ cup) long-grain rice

200 g (7 oz) minced (ground) chicken

¼ teaspoon ground allspice

1¼ teaspoons ground cinnamon

¼ teaspoon freshly ground black pepper

60 g (2¼ oz) unsalted shelled pistachio nuts

finely grated zest of 1 lemon

pinch of salt

4 tomatoes, sliced

4 garlic cloves, cut in half

1 bunch mint

1 litre (35 fl oz/4 cups) chicken stock

juice of 1 lemon

yoghurt, to serve

If you are using preserved vine leaves, soak them well, then rinse and pat them dry. Fresh vine leaves should first be blanched.

Wash the rice and mix it with the minced chicken, allspice, cinnamon, black pepper, pistachio nuts, lemon zest and the salt.

Lay a vine leaf on a work surface, vein side up, and place a spoonful of the rice filling across the base of the leaf. Roll it over once, fold the sides in and then continue to roll it into a neat sausage shape.

The dolmades should be around the size of your little finger — don't roll them too tightly or they will burst during cooking. Continue stuffing and rolling until the filling is all used.

Line the base of a heavy-based casserole dish with the remaining vine leaves and a layer of sliced tomatoes. Pack the dolmades in tightly on top of the tomatoes, stuffing the halved garlic cloves in among them. Lay the bunch of mint over the top, then pour in the chicken stock and lemon juice.

Cover with a plate and slowly bring to the boil. Once boiling, lower the heat and simmer gently for 45 minutes.

Turn out into a serving dish and serve hot, warm or even cold, with plenty of yoghurt.

Guy Grossi

Presented in 2004

Scallopini al limone

Serves 6

12 × 50 g (1¾ oz) slices veal
medallions

100 ml (3½ fl oz) olive oil

100 g (3½ oz/⅔ cup) plain
(all-purpose) flour

salt

200 ml (7 fl oz) white wine

50 ml (1¾ fl oz) lemon juice

50 g (1¾ oz) unsalted butter

Mashed potato

1 kg (2 lb 4 oz) potatoes, unpeeled

250 ml (9 fl oz/1 cup) milk

250 g (9 oz) butter,
diced and kept chilled

salt and pepper

To make the mashed potato, place the potatoes in a saucepan, covered with cold water. Sprinkle a generous amount of salt into the water. Bring the potatoes to a simmer and cook, uncovered, until a knife easily inserts into the potatoes. Drain the potatoes and peel them. Place the potatoes through a mouli into a large saucepan.

In a separate saucepan, add the milk and bring to the boil. Place the potatoes over medium heat and stir to slightly dry the potatoes. Turn the heat down and add the chilled butter, incorporating vigorously to obtain a smooth finish. Pour in the hot milk in an even stream, mixing until all the milk is absorbed. Season to taste with salt and pepper.

Place the veal slices between two sheets of plastic wrap and gently thin out the veal with a meat mallet.

Heat the olive oil in a large saucepan, dust both sides of the veal in the flour, place the veal in the saucepan and sauté on both sides. Season and deglaze with the white wine and lemon juice, bring to the boil, then remove the veal.

Add the butter to the pan and whisk into the sauce until amalgamated.

Arrange the veal on the plate and pour the sauce over. Serve with the mashed potato.

Cath Claringbold

Presented in 2002

Syrian roasted pumpkin and pickled date salad

Serves 4

Pickled dates

75 g (2⅔ oz) sumac, soaked in
450 ml (15½ fl oz) water overnight

250 g (9 oz) tamarind, (broken
into small pieces) soaked in
450 ml (15½ fl oz) water overnight

50 ml (1¾ fl oz) lemon juice

500 g (1 lb 2 oz) dates,
pitted and cut into 8

2 garlic cloves, crushed

1 teaspoon salt

¼ teaspoon each of freshly ground
black pepper, ground cinnamon
and ground nutmeg

Roasted pumpkin

½ small Jap pumpkin (winter squash)

50 ml (1¾ fl oz) olive oil,
plus extra for drizzling

2 red onions

1 teaspoon pomegranate molasses
(available from Middle Eastern grocers)

juice of 1 lemon

200 g (7 oz) wild rocket (arugula)

35 g (1¼ oz/¼ cup) walnuts, toasted
and skins removed

¼ cup pickled dates (see recipe above)

100 g (3½ oz) good-quality goat's curd

Pickled dates

Strain the sumac and tamarind through fine sieves and discard the solids. Mix the liquid together with the lemon juice and bring to the boil in a saucepan. Add the remaining ingredients and bring to a slight simmer. Pour into jars, cool, seal and stand for 1 week before using.

Roasted pumpkin

Preheat the oven to 180°C (350°F/Gas 4). Peel the pumpkin and remove the seeds. Cut the flesh into small uniform pieces, season with salt and freshly ground black pepper. Drizzle with the olive oil and roast for 20 minutes, depending on the size, or until tender.

Peel the onions and cut into small wedges. Cook using the same process as the pumpkin. The onion should be soft but not too coloured.

Make a vinaigrette using the pomegranate molasses, lemon juice and 50 ml of olive oil. Season with salt and pepper.

When the vegetables are cooked, toss together with the vinaigrette. Gently mix through the wild rocket, walnuts and pickled dates. Finish the salad with small spoonfuls of goat's curd, dotted across the top. Serve immediately.

Alister Brown

Presented in 2003

Sautéed Cervena venison fillet with shiitake mushrooms and black cherry relish

Serves 8 as a starter

Black cherry relish

1 kg (2 lb 4 oz) black cherries, pitted

20 g (¾ oz) fresh ginger, minced

60 g (2¼ oz) fresh shallot, minced

170 ml (5½ fl oz/⅔ cup) sherry vinegar

165 g (5¾ oz/¾ cup) sugar

1 teaspoon mixed spice

salt and freshly ground white pepper

Confit garlic

100 g (3½ oz) garlic cloves, peeled

2 fresh bay leaves

1 sprig thyme

1 sprig rosemary

250 ml (9 fl oz/1 cup) olive oil

Black cherry relish

In a non-reactive saucepan, place the whole pitted cherries, ginger, shallot, sherry vinegar, sugar and mixed spice. Place the saucepan over medium–low heat and cook for 2 hours or until the cherries start to break down and you have a slightly wet, jam-like consistency. Cool to room temperature. Season with salt and pepper to taste. Preserve in sterilised jars or refrigerate until required.

Confit garlic

Preheat the oven to 160°C (315°F/Gas 2–3). Take a small suitable ovenproof dish, spread out the garlic cloves and top with the bay leaves, thyme and rosemary. Pour over the olive oil, then cover with foil. Place in the oven and check after 30 minutes. The garlic should still be whole but soft all the way through. Store submerged in the oil until required.

To assemble

unsalted butter and olive oil,
for cooking

200 g (7 oz) fresh shiitake
mushrooms, stalks removed

fresh thyme, finely chopped

fresh sage, finely chopped

a few confit garlic cloves
(see recipe opposite)

1 × 1 kg (2 lb 4 oz) piece Cervena
venison fillet

To serve

80 ml (2½ fl oz/⅓ cup)
demi-glace, warmed

black cherry relish
(see recipe opposite)

porcini (cep) oil, for drizzling

To assemble

Take a sauté pan and bring up to medium heat. Add a little butter and oil, then drop in your mushrooms, thyme and sage. Sauté for 2 minutes or until the mushrooms begin to caramelise. Add a few confit garlic cloves and season with salt and pepper. Cook for another minute, then remove from the heat and keep warm.

Heat a skillet or sauté pan to medium–high heat. Season the venison fillet with salt and pepper. Pour a little olive oil in the pan, then immediately add the fillet. Sauté until golden on all sides, but no longer than 2 minutes. Remove from the pan and leave to rest for 3–4 minutes.

To serve

Take 8 hot entrée plates and divide the mushrooms evenly in a pile on each plate. Slice the venison fillet and arrange next to the mushrooms. Pour over a little preheated demi-glace, top with a small amount of cherry relish, then finally drizzle over a little porcini oil.
Serve immediately.

Janni Kyritsis

Presented in 1999

Diples

(Deep-fried pastries)

Makes about 50 pieces

Pastries

3 eggs

2 tablespoons orange juice

60 ml (2 fl oz/¼ cup) olive oil

360 g (12¾ oz) plain
(all-purpose) flour

½ teaspoon baking powder

olive oil, for deep-frying

toasted sesame seeds,
for sprinkling

Syrup

700 g (1 lb 9 oz/2 cups) honey

250 ml (9 fl oz/1 cup) water

2 strips orange zest

To make the syrup, bring all the ingredients to the boil, then cool.

To make the pastries, whisk the eggs until thick. Gradually add the juice and olive oil.

Combine the flour and baking powder and sift into a bowl. Add the egg mixture. Knead until smooth. Rest for 1 hour. Roll out as thin as possible by hand or use a pasta machine.

Cut into 20 cm × 1 cm (8 × ½ inch) ribbons.

Roll loosely around your finger, then remove, hold it with a fork and deep-fry in hot oil. Drain on paper towel.

While still hot, dip the diples in the syrup and sprinkle with the toasted sesame seeds.

Frank Camorra

Herminda's empanada de maiz

(Corn pie with baby scallops)

Makes 10 media raciones (serves 10)

80 ml (2½ fl oz/⅓ cup) extra virgin olive oil

2 leeks, white part only, trimmed and halved lengthways, thinly sliced

6 garlic cloves, thinly sliced

3 fresh bay leaves

1 green capsicum (pepper), deseeded, membrane removed, finely diced

1½ tablespoons real cornflour (cornstarch)

300 ml (10½ fl oz) albariño wine

400 g (14 oz) baby scallops, cleaned from their shells, liquid reserved

1 small handful of curly-leaf parsley, chopped

Heat the olive oil in a large heavy-based saucepan over medium–high heat. Add the sliced leeks and cook for 5 minutes or until they begin to brown. Add the garlic, bay leaves, capsicum and a pinch of salt, reduce the heat to medium and cook for 15 minutes or until the capsicum is soft. Increase the heat to high, add the cornflour, cook for 2 minutes while stirring, then add the wine and let it bubble for a few minutes. Add 300 ml (10½ fl oz) of water and bring to a simmer.

Reduce the heat to medium and cook for 40 minutes or until you have a rich thick ragoût. Add the scallops and their juice. Stir in the parsley, check the seasoning, then remove from the heat and cool.

Meanwhile, to make the pastry, place all the dry ingredients, a pinch of salt and the yeast into a large bowl. Add the olive oil and 500 ml (17 fl oz/2 cups) of just-boiled water. Stir using a wooden spoon. The dough should be very dry and feel like it isn't coming together. Some flour may remain unincorporated. Place the dough in a lightly oiled bowl, then cover and stand in a warm place for 30 minutes.

Pastry

280 g (10 oz) plain (all purpose) flour

560 g (1 lb 4¼ oz) coarse polenta

90 g (3¼ oz) roasted corn, finely ground

160 g (5⅔ oz) rye flour

40 g (1½ oz) fresh yeast (or 20 g/¾ oz dried active yeast)

100 ml (3½ fl oz) extra virgin olive oil, plus extra for brushing

1 egg, lightly beaten

Preheat the oven to 180°C (350°F/Gas 4). Lightly brush a 15 cm × 25 cm (6 x 10 inch) baking tray with olive oil.

Take a large handful of pastry and roll out on a well-floured surface until 2 mm (¹⁄₁₆ inch) thick. Place on the baking tray and repeat with another handful of pastry until the tray is covered with pastry, using your fingers to fill in any holes in the pastry.

Spread the cooled filling over the pastry, leaving a 1 cm (½ inch) border. Using your fingers, coarsely crumble the remaining pastry over the filling to create a rough textured layer over the top. Brush the top with the lightly beaten egg, drizzle with the extra virgin olive oil, then bake for 15 minutes.

Remove the pie from the oven and, using a small knife and spoon, break up the pastry topping into fine crumbs and spread evenly over the top. Return to the oven and cook for another 15 minutes or until the base is cooked and the top has the appearance and texture of dry earth. Serve warm or at room temperature.

As always, an amazing range of international chefs who all seem totally comfortable in delivering their knowledge and are entertaining. It's definitely a time of year I look forward to being involved in and eating my way through. FRANK CAMORRA, 2010

Big Night Event, George
Parade Laneway 2008.

Streets and Laneways

One of the distinct strengths of the Melbourne Food and Wine Festival has been its ability to pinpoint the things that are uniquely Melbourne. Little wonder then that the Festival has spent much of its time hunting for treasures on Melbourne's food streets and in the recesses of the CBD's labyrinth of hidden laneways because this is a city that likes a secret location and an undiscovered gem — the Turkish bakery hidden among a cluster of dress shops on Sydney Road or the tiny Chinese restaurant in an alley in Chinatown that does brilliant dim sum. Of course the Festival didn't invent places like these but by bringing them to more people's attention, showing the locals what they've got, it has ensured that these unique places have become more tightly woven into the fabric of the city.

A popular and enduring feature of each year's Festival is the program of tours and "crawls" that take people to places in their own city where they may never have been before. These food exploration tours have been part of the program since the first Festival when food writer and cooking teacher Meera Freeman took groups of people to explore the Vietnamese sights, sounds and flavours on Victoria Street in Richmond.

It was also in 1993 that the Festival shone the spotlight on the idea of a "food street". Being a festival with quite exacting standards, a street didn't qualify for the title "food street" just because it had a couple of shops that fit the bill. According to that year's program, a "food street" was one that had cafes that "don't blink an eye when you order a double macchiato", restaurants, a wine bar or two "with a good selection by the glass", breakfast any time of the day, specialty providores like butchers, fruiterers, delis and wine shops and, preferably "a good bookshop or two". There were four streets deemed to have qualified that year — Lygon, Chapel, Acland and Brunswick streets — that were turned into food-themed piazzas for a day.

The idea of tours and food streets continued in subsequent Festivals but, with each year, the scope of these events became more specialised, with chef Greg Malouf revealing the Middle Eastern treasures on Sydney Road, restaurant owner John Dunham guiding people through the incredible variety that is the Footscray Market, and Giancarlo Giusti giving insiders a point of view of the Little Italy of Lygon Street.

One of the longest-running events in the Festival program, and one that has spawned a whole genre is the Duck Crawl. First appearing in 1997 as the brainchild of wine industry stalwart Roy Moorfield, the Duck Crawl took people through Chinatown, matching the various versions of duck, from Peking to tea-smoked, with Australian pinot noir. It's still a feature of the Festival today (running over several sessions due to popular demand), has been imitated world-wide and become an inspiration for similar events in Melbourne including a Crab Crawl, Noodle Crawl, Dumpling Crawl, Carnivorous Crawl, Rhône Crawl and, possibly the most literal, the Martini Crawl.

The Melbourne Food and Wine Festival has also been a long-term supporter of Melbourne's renowned small-bar culture. Most commonly found in hidden locations down lanes, up stairs or in basements, the small Melbourne-style bar was unheard of when the Festival first kicked off but by 1998 there were bar-themed events in the program that embraced the tucked-away cocktail culture that Melburnians had so quickly embraced and adopted.

Melbourne's laneways have also been used for dinners and parties, the first being an Italian feast held in George Parade. In 2010 a "Laneways & Rooftops" event saw a series of dinners — Vietnamese, French and Italian feasts, an Aphrodisiac Orgy at Madame Brussels, a barbecue on a St Kilda rooftop — that highlighted just how much a part of Melbourne life these once unused and neglected spaces have become.

For 10 years the Gala Dinner, supported by Crown, has been held in often unlikely locations (a television studio, a warehouse, in sheds at Docklands and in meat and produce markets) and has seen chefs such as Antonio Carluccio, Shannon Bennett, Atul Kochhar, Chris Salans, Nobu Matsuhisa, Thierry Marx and Fergus Henderson bring delicious life to these hidden and obscure locations. It is interesting to see now the number of food tours highlighting all sorts of cuisine, produce and themes running through Melbourne's streets and laneways all year round. There was almost nothing like it when the Festival first came to town, but now it is yet another example of how deeply integrated the Festival has become with the culinary life of a food-mad city.

Clockwise from top left: A Spanish Affair, Comme, 2009; Open House, St Ali, 2010; Joie de Vivre, Comme, 2010; Night of the Coq, Libertine, 2009; A Spanish Affair at Comme, 2009; Open House, St Ali, 2010.

Donovan Cooke

Presented in 1999

Torte of slippery jack and pine mushrooms

Serves 4

Chicken mousse

3 chicken breasts

5 egg whites

250 ml (9 fl oz/1 cup) thickened (whipping) cream

salt and cayenne pepper

Herb pancakes

400 ml (14 fl oz) milk

2 eggs

125 g (4½ oz) plain (all-purpose) flour

1 tablespoon chopped chives

Filling

8 medium pine mushrooms, stalks trimmed, caps diced

1 bunch chives, finely chopped

1 teaspoon chopped truffle (optional)

1 tablespoon truffle oil

12 large slippery jack mushrooms, stalks trimmed

Chicken mousse

To make the chicken mousse, put the bowl of a food processor in the refrigerator until cold. Trim the skin from the chicken breasts. Pulse the meat in the chilled bowl of the food processor until blended. Incorporate the egg white and pulse again until shiny. Put the mixture into a clean bowl. Place the bowl over a second bowl holding ice cubes and beat in the cream. Season with salt and cayenne pepper. Make a quenelle-shaped tester of the mousse and poach to check the seasoning. The mousse should be fairly firm. Refrigerate until needed.

Herb pancakes

To make the herb pancakes, blend or whisk the milk, eggs and flour together. Strain, season, then add the chives. Rest in the refrigerator for 20 minutes before cooking.

Add enough batter to coat a small non-stick frying pan. Cook until lightly golden, then flip and cook for another 30 seconds. You will need 8 pancakes.

Filling

Fold the pine mushrooms through the chilled chicken mousse along with the chives, chopped truffle and truffle oil. Season with salt and pepper.

On each pancake, smear 1 tablespoon of the mousse and top with a slippery jack, then another tablespoon of mousse and another slippery jack, then repeat once more so you have 3 slippery jacks layered on each pancake. Fold the pancake around the filling to make a neat parcel. Refrigerate while you make the sauce.

Madeira sauce

1 kg (2 lb 4 oz) chicken wings, chopped into small pieces

vegetable oil, for cooking

10 shallots, sliced

200 g (7 oz) button mushrooms, sliced

1 bulb garlic, roughly chopped

1 tablespoon sherry vinegar

375 ml (13 fl oz/1½ cups) Madeira

1 litre (35 fl oz/4 cups) veal stock

1 litre (35 fl oz/4 cups) chicken stock

1 fresh bay leaf

1 sprig thyme

2 tablespoons pouring (single) cream

50 g (1¾ oz) butter

Tortes

500 g (1 lb 2 oz) puff pastry

1 egg yolk, lightly whisked, for eggwash

Madeira sauce

To make the Madeira sauce, sauté the chicken wings in hot vegetable oil until golden brown. Drain the wings in a colander. Sweat the shallots and mushrooms in some vegetable oil in a heavy-based saucepan, add the garlic and allow to colour slightly. Deglaze the pan with sherry vinegar, add the Madeira and reduce by half. Add the chicken wings, stocks and herbs. Cook this gently for 1 hour. Strain the stock, return to the pan and reduce by half again. Whisk in the cream and butter. Season with salt and pepper. When ready to serve, bring back to the boil.

Tortes

Cut the puff pastry into 4 rectangle pieces. Lightly flour a work surface, then roll out the pastry pieces to a thickness of 3 mm (⅛ inch). Cut each rectangle in half and place the mushroom parcels on half of the pastry rectangles. Brush around the parcels with a little eggwash, then place the remaining pastry rectangles on top, pressing down carefully to seal. Refrigerate until firm.

Preheat the oven to 220°C (425°F/Gas 7).

When the puff pastry rectangles are firm, using a sharp knife, trim the pastry to create a nice shape. Using the tip of the knife, score a pattern on top of the tortes. Glaze the tortes with more eggwash and bake for 12–15 minutes.

To serve

Cut the tortes in half using a serrated knife. Place 2 halves each on 4 warmed plates. Serve with the Madeira sauce.

Tony Tan

Presented in 1999

Eurasian gammon curry

Serves 4–6 as part of a shared meal

Similar to a vindaloo from Goa, the prunes, gammon and olives from the shores of southern Europe are not only surprising but they marry splendidly with the seasonings of southern Indian cooking. This is one of the vestiges of the colonial era. This "curry" is cooked by the Portuguese community of Melaka and the Eurasian community of Singapore. It owes its origin to the Portuguese vinho d'alhos.

500 g (1 lb 2 oz) gammon
10 large dried red chillies
1 tablespoon cumin seeds, toasted and ground
150 ml (5 fl oz) vegetable oil
200 ml (7 fl oz) red wine vinegar
1 sprig curry leaves
1 teaspoon fenugreek
1 teaspoon brown mustard seeds
1 onion, minced
½ cup Kalamata olives
2 medium tomatoes, deseeded and chopped
105 g (3⅔ oz/½ cup) pitted prunes
sugar, to taste

Cut the gammon into 3 cm (1¼ inch) cubes. Soak in cold water for 15–20 minutes if very salty. Otherwise omit this step.

Soak the dried chillies in hot water to soften, then process the chillies with a little water to a paste. Mix the chillies with the ground cumin seeds. Fry the paste with 50 ml (1¾ fl oz) of the oil over low heat until aromatic. Remove the paste from the pan and combine with the vinegar. Pour the chilli–vinegar mixture over the gammon and marinate for 2 hours.

Heat the rest of the oil in a large, deep-sided frying pan over medium heat and fry the curry leaves, fenugreek and mustard seeds quickly. Do not burn the aromatic seeds. Add the onion and fry until fragrant.

Drain the gammon and reserve the marinade. Add the drained gammon to the pan and seal. Add the olives, tomato and reserved marinade with sufficient water to cover. Simmer the curry until the meat is tender, 40–60 minutes.

Ten minutes before the curry is ready, add the prunes. Taste and add sugar if desired. Serve with steamed rice.

Presented in 2010

Braised short rib with soy apple marinade, apples and pears

Serves 8

Short ribs

2⅔ cups water

½ cup usukuchi (light soy sauce), plus 2 tablespoons

3 tablespoons pear juice, plus 1 teaspoon

3 tablespoons apple juice, plus 1 teaspoon

2½ tablespoons mirin

1 tablespoon Asian sesame oil

1¼ cups sugar

10 grinds black pepper

½ small onion

1 small carrot

3 spring onions (scallions), white part only

2 garlic cloves

8 pieces bone-in short ribs (140–170 g/5–6 oz each), trimmed of any silverskin and cut into individual ribs

3 apples, peeled, cored and quartered

3 pears, peeled, cored and quartered

To make the marinade for the short ribs, combine the water, usukuchi, pear and apple juices, mirin, sesame oil, sugar, pepper, onion, carrot, spring onion and garlic in a large saucepan and bring to the boil over high heat. Reduce the heat so the liquid simmers gently and cook for 10 minutes. Strain the solids out of the marinade and cool it in the refrigerator. It can be stored, covered, for up to a few days.

Combine each short rib with ½ cup marinade and some apples and pears in a vacuum-sealable bag and seal it, then seal in a second bag. (If one of those bags pops, your rib is toast, and it'll make a mess of everything, so better safe than sorry.) Put the bagged ribs in a water bath and set your immersion circulator to 60°C (140°F). Cook the ribs at that temperature for 48 hours.

When the ribs are cooked, remove them from the warm water bath and plunge them — still in their bags — into a large bowl of icy cold water. After they've been cooled, they can be stored in the refrigerator for up to a few days or frozen for a few weeks (defrost them overnight in the refrigerator).

Cut the ribs and fruit out of their bags over a mixing bowl to catch the braising liquid; set the ribs and fruit aside.

Strain the braising liquid through a fine-mesh sieve into a small saucepan. Bring it to the boil over high heat and reduce it until you have about 2 cups, no more than 10 minutes. Reserve, covered (in the pan is fine), until you're ready to plate the dish.

Meanwhile, slide the bones out of the short ribs. Trim off any large obvious pieces of fat, and trim the ribs into neat cubes (or rectangles) that weigh about 85 g (3 oz) each.

Garnish

8 spring onions (scallions)

grapeseed or other neutral oil
or rendered pork or duck fat,
for deep-frying

dashi-braised daikon
(see recipe below)

¼ cup pickled mustard seeds
(see recipe below)

sea salt

Dashi-braised daikon

2 medium daikon (white radish),
each a little more than 2.5 cm
(1 inch) in diameter

4 cups dashi (homemade
or instant)

Pickled mustard seeds

1 cup yellow mustard seeds

1½ cups water

1½ cups rice wine vinegar

½ cup sugar

1 tablespoon sea salt

To make the garnish, bring a small saucepan of salted water to the boil. Add the spring onion and blanch for 10 seconds, then drain and cool in an ice bath or under cold running water. Drain well and reserve.

Heat a litre or two of oil to 180˚C (350˚F) in a high-sided pan over medium–high heat. Line a plate with a double thickness of paper towel on which to drain the beef. Fry the short rib chunks in batches as necessary, so as not to crowd the pan, for 3–4 minutes; they should be mahogany brown outside and warmed all the way through. Remove the fried rib chunks from the oil and drain on the paper towel for a couple of minutes.

To make the dashi-braised daikon, scrub the daikon, peel it and cut it into 2.5 cm (1 inch) thick discs. Bring the dashi to a steady simmer in a small saucepan on the stove. Add the daikon and simmer for 30 minutes or until it is tender but not falling apart. At this point, you can cool the daikon in the dashi and store it in the refrigerator for up to 1 day, until ready to use. When you're ready to serve, bring the dashi back up to a simmer and hold it there until the daikon is warmed through, about 5 minutes. Scoop the daikon out of the dashi to serve. (The dashi can be reserved for another use or discarded.)

To make the pickled mustard seeds, combine the mustard seeds, water, vinegar, sugar and salt in a small saucepan and bring to the gentlest of simmers over low heat. Cook the mustard seeds, stirring often, until they're plump and tender, about 45 minutes. If the seeds look to be drying out, add water as needed to keep them barely submerged. Cool and store in a covered container in the refrigerator. Pickled mustard seeds will keep for months. Makes 1 cup.

To serve, put a couple of tablespoons of the reduced braising liquid in the centre of each of 8 large white plates. Lay a piece of apple and a piece of pear across the pool of liquid (cut the fruit lengthways in half if they're thick) and nestle a braised daikon disc up against it. Lay the green part of the blanched spring onion across the fruit (the white should be sticking out like the minute hand on a clock). Slice the chunks of short ribs into 4 cm (1½ inch) thick slices each, and shingle them over the spring onion green. Fold/wrap the spring onion back around over the meat, carefully perch the mustard seeds atop the daikon, and sprinkle the meat with sea salt. Serve at once.

From *Momofuku*, David Chang and Peter Meehan, Clarkson Potter
(a division of Random House Inc) (2009).

Guy Grossi

Presented in 2004

Calamari in padella

(Pan-fried calamari with baked tomato)

Serves 4

A quick simple dish with great flavour return.

8 large roma (plum) tomatoes, cored, halved and deseeded

handful of parsley stalks

2 fresh bay leaves

6 peppercorns

sea salt and freshly ground black pepper

75 ml (2⅓ fl oz) olive oil, plus extra for drizzling

800 g (1 lb 12 oz) fresh calamari, cleaned and cut into 3 cm (1¼ inch) pieces

plain (all-purpose) flour, for dusting

100 g (3½ oz) peas

2 garlic cloves, finely chopped

1 chilli, finely chopped

8 basil leaves, torn

juice of ½ lemon

3 tablespoons flat-leaf (Italian) parsley leaves, chopped

Preheat the oven to 120°C (235°F/Gas ½). Place the tomatoes in a deep, small baking tray and add the parsley stalks, bay leaves and peppercorns. Season with salt and pepper before drizzling with the olive oil. Roast in the oven. Allow the tomatoes to cook until the oil starts to bubble and the tomatoes become tender. Remove them from the oven and drain off the oil. Slice in half.

In a large frying pan, heat the 75 ml of olive oil and allow it to become hot before adding the calamari. While the oil is heating up, place the flour in a tray and lightly dust the calamari. Add the calamari to the pan and cook until golden in colour. Add the peas, garlic, chilli and basil leaves and cook until the garlic has gone golden. Season with salt and pepper and the lemon juice, then add in some of the chopped parsley.

In a separate pan, heat up the tomato so that it is hot. Arrange in the middle of each plate, top with the fried calamari, drizzle some olive oil around the plate and garnish with the remaining parsley.

Mirka at Tolarno Hotel.

Raymond Capaldi

Presented in 1998

Confit of Atlantic salmon with basil potato mash, ox cheek and lemon thyme jus

Serves 4

Braised ox cheeks

2 kg (4 lb 8 oz) beef cheeks

125 ml (4 fl oz/½ cup) extra virgin olive oil, plus extra for drizzling

6 cloves garlic, roughly chopped

rind of 1 orange, peeled in strips

3 sprigs rosemary

10 small fresh bay leaves

500 ml (17 fl oz/2 cups) good red wine

2 large onions, roughly chopped

2 stalks celery, roughly chopped

sea salt flakes and freshly ground black pepper

500 ml (17 fl oz/2 cups) reduced beef stock

Red wine French shallots

100 g (3½ oz) French shallots (eschalots), peeled

Ox cheek and lemon thyme jus

100 g (3½ oz) braised ox cheek, cut into 1 cm (½ inch) pieces

lemon juice, to taste

30 lemon thyme leaves

50 g (1¾ oz) chilled butter, cubed

The day before cooking the braised ox cheeks, toss the beef cheeks in a little of the olive oil with the garlic cloves, orange rind, rosemary and bay leaves. Cover and refrigerate overnight to marinate.

Preheat the oven to 120°C. Drizzle the beef cheeks with 60ml (2 fl oz/ ¼ cup) of the olive oil and season with salt and pepper. Heat a frying pan over medium heat, then brown the cheeks on each side and place in a heavy-based casserole. Deglaze the frying pan with the red wine then reduce by half and add to the casserole. Wipe out the frying pan, add the remaining olive oil and cook the onions and celery until browned. Season with sea salt and pepper and transfer to the casserole.

Add the beef stock and place the covered casserole in the oven. Turn the beef cheeks frequently. Check after 3 hours — depending on their size and the breed of cattle, they may take up to 6 hours to become tender. Remove the lid for the final 2 hours of cooking. Remove the cheeks from the braising liquid and set aside.

To make the red wine French shallots, transfer the ox cheeks braising liquid to a saucepan, add the French shallots and simmer until reduced to 800 ml (28 fl oz). Set aside.

To make the ox cheek and lemon thyme jus, place the beef cheek pieces in a small saucepan, add a little reduced braising liquid from the red wine French shallots, and set aside.

Chlorophyll

100 g (3½ oz) picked English
spinach, washed

1 small handful of basil leaves

1 tablespoon olive oil

Basil potato mash

250 g (9 oz) desiree potatoes

1 small handful of coarse rock salt

25 ml (¾ fl oz) milk

50 ml (1¾ fl oz) double
(thick) cream

50 g (1¾ oz) unsalted butter

freshly grated nutmeg, to taste

caramelised lemon zest, to taste

basil oil, to taste

Confit

350 ml (12 fl oz) melted goose or
duck fat

1 sprig rosemary

1 sprig thyme

1 strip lemon zest

1 strip orange zest

1 garlic clove

4 × 180 g (6¼ oz) Atlantic salmon
fillets, pin-boned and skin removed

To serve

20 lemon thyme flowers

sea salt, for sprinkling

To make the chlorophyll, blanch the spinach and basil in a saucepan of boiling water for 30 seconds, then drain and refresh in iced water. Drain again, then squeeze out as much water as possible from the leaves. Purée the leaves with the oil until smooth.

To make the basil potato mash, preheat the oven to 180°C (350°F/ Gas 4). Place the whole potatoes on a bed of rock salt and bake for 30 minutes or until tender.

While the potatoes are baking, make the confit. Heat the goose or duck fat in a saucepan until boiling, then add the rosemary, thyme, lemon zest, orange zest and garlic clove. Place the pan above or beside the stove until the temperature of the fat reaches 45°C (113°F). As soon as the fat reaches 45°C, season the salmon then, place in the fat and stand for 10–15 minutes. (The time will depend on the thickness of the salmon pieces but you want them to be pink in the middle.)

To finish the potato mash, take the potatoes from the oven. While still hot, squeeze them out of their skins, then pass the flesh through a fine sieve into a large bowl. (Don't use a food processor or the potatoes will be gluey. You can wear rubber gloves while squeezing the potatoes if you like.) Bring the milk, cream, butter and nutmeg just to the boil in a small saucepan, then add to the hot mashed potato. At the last minute, add the chlorophyll. If it splits, fold 2 teaspoons of cold water to the mixture. Add the caramelised lemon zest and basil oil and season to taste. Set aside and keep warm.

When the salmon is ready, heat up the French shallots and the braised ox cheek. Add a little lemon juice and the lemon thyme to the ox cheek and whisk in the cold butter, a cube at a time, until emulsified.

To serve, place some of the potato mash in the middle of each plate and place a piece of salmon on top. Pour the ox cheek jus and red wine French shallots around the mash. Scatter with the lemon thyme flowers and a little salt and serve.

Shannon Bennett

Presented in 2003

Mushroom risotto

Serves 8

The recipe involves the convenient step of pre-cooking the rice; this can be done well in advance of the final completion of the recipe. Store the pre-cooked rice well covered in the fridge.

Risotto

1 onion, finely chopped

50 ml (1¾ fl oz) good-quality olive oil

250 g (9 oz) arborio rice

350 ml (12 fl oz) white wine

250 ml (9 fl oz/1 cup) chicken stock

300 ml (10½ fl oz) mushroom stock *(see page 66)*

50 g (1¾ oz) frozen or 20 g (¾ oz) dried ceps (porcini), chopped (if using dried, soak in hot water for 30 minutes, then drain)

acid butter *(see page 66)*

60 g (2¼ oz) Grana Padano parmesan, grated

1 bunch tarragon, leaves picked, washed and chopped

continued >

Sweat the onion in the olive oil over low–medium heat. Add the rice, stirring until each grain of rice is coated with oil. Deglaze with the white wine and cook out until dry, stirring the rice with a wooden spoon to prevent sticking. Add the chicken stock and cook for approximately 5 minutes or until dry, stirring occasionally. Lay the rice out on a tray, cover with plastic wrap and refrigerate (see Note).

Bring the mushroom stock to the boil.

Add the cooked rice to a suitably heavy-based saucepan. Measure 2 tablespoons per serve for an entrée or 3 tablespoons for a light main course.

Add the hot mushroom stock to the level of the rice in the saucepan. Add the chopped ceps, then simmer over a gentle heat until the rice has absorbed all the stock.

Add ½ tablespoon of the acid butter per tablespoon of rice. I know it sounds like a lot but this gives the rice its licence to change from a sort of rice pilaf into a creamy risotto. Add a good pinch of parmesan and gently fold through with the acid butter. The transformation is complete. If the risotto appears a little firm, add more mushroom stock to it to loosen the texture. Season and add the tarragon. Serve immediately.

Note: The rice at this stage is now pre-cooked and can be stored in the fridge ready for the final cooking procedure. Alternatively, you can continue on with the recipe without cooling.

The enthusiasm from all the chefs is incredible. There's no ego involved, there's just a lot of learning by us [the local chefs] and them [the visiting chefs]. SHANNON BENNETT, 2010

Acid butter

2 tablespoons Champagne vinegar

80 ml (2½ fl oz/⅓ cup) white wine

1 French shallot (eschalot), thinly sliced

1 teaspoon thyme

1 fresh bay leaf

500 g (1 lb 2 oz) cultured butter, chopped

Mushroom stock

1 kg (2 lb 4 oz) button, Paris or wild mushrooms, thinly sliced

350 ml (12 fl oz) R.L. Buller & Son Fine Old Malmsey or Madeira wine

350 ml (12 fl oz) white wine

2 French shallots (eschalots), trimmed and sliced

½ bulb garlic

6 sprigs thyme

1 fresh bay leaf

5 black peppercorns

1 litre (35 fl oz/4 cups) chicken or vegetable stock

Acid butter

Reduce the vinegar and white wine with the shallot, thyme and bay leaf by four-fifths. Strain the solids, then return the liquid to the pan over medium heat. Whisk in the butter to form a beurre blanc-style sauce. Pass through a fine sieve into a storable container and refrigerate until firm.

Mushroom stock

Add all the ingredients to a stockpot and boil rapidly for 1 hour. The stock will remain relatively clear due to the second-class protein properties in the mushrooms, which makes the stock a great base for any broth or clear soup. Taste the stock; if satisfied the mushrooms have imparted enough flavour and colour, remove from the heat and strain through a fine chinois or sieve.

Place the strained stock back into the stockpot and reduce by one-third. The stock can be easily stored in the freezer for future use. Makes about 750 ml (26 fl oz/3 cups).

From Bistro Vue, Melbourne.

Guy Grossi

Presented in 2010

Briased Chianina, Chianti, porcini and polenta

Serves 6

100 ml (3½ fl oz) olive oil

3 onions, thinly sliced

3 garlic cloves, crushed

30 g (1 oz) dried porcini, soaked in warm water for 1 hour

2 fresh bay leaves

3 tablespoons chopped sage

2 tablespoons chopped parsley

½ teaspoon ground cloves

½ teaspoon ground star anise

180 g (6 oz) tomato paste (concentrated purée)

400 ml (14 fl oz) Chianti

1.2 kg (2 lb 10 oz) Chianina beef shin, cut into 60 g (2¼ oz) pieces

sea salt and freshly ground pepper

1.5 litres (52 fl oz) beef stock

Polenta

sea salt

2 litres (70 fl oz) water

350 g (12 oz) polenta

100 g (3½ oz) grated parmesan

20 g (¾ oz) butter

Heat 60 ml (2 fl oz/¼ cup) of the oil in a saucepan large enough to hold the beef, and cook the onion and garlic over medium–high heat for 5 minutes or until the onion starts to caramelise.

Lift out the porcini from the soaking liquid and add to the onion along with the herbs and spices and mix in. Add the tomato paste and cook for 2 minutes, then deglaze with the Chianti, reduce the heat to low and simmer gently.

Heat a large frying pan with the remaining oil and brown the meat on all sides for 5 minutes, seasoning with salt and pepper. Add the browned meat to the sauce and cover with the stock. Bring to a simmer, reduce the heat to low and continue simmering gently for 1½–2 hours. Take a piece of meat out of the sauce and cut to taste for tenderness. Check the seasoning.

To make the polenta, salt the water and bring it to the boil in a large saucepan. Add the polenta in a steady stream, stirring constantly. When all the polenta has been added, stir for 2–3 minutes, then reduce the heat to low and simmer for 15–20 minutes, stirring occasionally. Stir in the parmesan and the butter, season to taste and serve immediately.

Place a spoonful of the polenta to the side of a main-course plate, arrange the meat on the other side and spoon the sauce over the top of the meat.

Roy Choi

Presented in 2011

Salsa verde

Makes about 3 cups

60 ml (2 fl oz/¼ cup) aji mirin *(see Note)*

125 ml (4 fl oz/½ cup) natural rice wine vinegar

½ bunch mint, leaves picked

½ bunch coriander (cilantro), stems and all, washed and roughly chopped

6 sprigs Thai basil, leaves picked

2½ garlic cloves

½ shallot

1½ serrano chillies

1½ jalapeño chillies

juice of 1 lime

1½ tablespoons sesame seeds, toasted

1½ tomatillos, washed

2 pinches of sea salt

pinch of freshly ground white pepper

125 ml (4 fl oz/½ cup) canola oil

125 ml (4 fl oz/½ cup) extra virgin olive oil

Purée all the ingredients in a blender till smooth, adding the oils slowly.

Note: Aji mirin contains salt and corn syrup to help stabilise its viscosity.

The Melbourne Food and Wine festival is a true pioneer and America might just want to take notice! Melbourne is the world's best kept secret and the food scene in Melbourne is off the charts. ROY CHOI, 2011

Greg Malouf

Presented in 1996

Syrian cigar nut pastries with orange–honey cream

Serves 8

To make the sugar syrup, place all the ingredients, apart from the orange blossom water, into a stainless steel saucepan and slowly bring to the boil. Continue boiling for 3 minutes. Remove from the heat and allow to cool down. Before refrigerating, add the orange blossom water.

To make the cigars, preheat the oven to 180°C (350°F/Gas 4).

In a stainless steel bowl, mix the crushed walnuts, almonds and pistachio nuts together with the brown sugar and orange blossom water.

Place one sheet of filo pastry on a dry surface, lightly brush with the melted butter and sprinkle 1 tablespoon of the nut mixture evenly all over the sheet.

Place a long knitting needle, metal skewer or chopstick at the short end of the pastry and roll up the filo around the knitting needle as evenly as possible. Push the ends of the filo towards each other so that the pastry slides along the needle and scrunches up in an even manner. Pull out the needle and lay the cigar on a buttered baking tray. Repeat with the remaining sheets of filo.

Bake for 20–25 minutes or until browned all over. Remove from the oven and place on a wire rack. Brush with the sugar syrup while hot, then refrigerate.

To make the orange–honey cream, whip the cream with the honey and orange zest until firm.

To assemble, cut the cigars on an angle in half, trimming the ends also. Place 4 cigar pieces in the centre of a plate to form a box. Spoon the orange–honey cream into the centre of the box and drizzle some sugar syrup all over.

Sugar syrup

200 g (7 oz) sugar

100 ml (3½ fl oz) water

1 cinnamon stick

2 cardamom pods, lightly crushed

2 teaspoons orange blossom water

Cigars

50 g (1¾ oz) crushed walnuts

50 g (1¾ oz) crushed almonds

50 g (1¾ oz) crushed pistachio nuts

100 g (3½ oz) soft brown sugar

2 teaspoons orange blossom water

16 sheets filo pastry

250 g (9 oz) unsalted butter, melted

Orange–honey cream

250 ml (9 fl oz/1 cup) pouring (single) cream

finely grated zest of ½ orange

50 ml (1¾ fl oz) honey

Philippe Mouchel

Presented in 2011

Red fruits and lemon mirliton tart

Serves 6

250 g (9 oz/2 cups) frozen berries

icing (confectioner's) sugar and fresh berries, to serve

fresh berry coulis and berry sorbet, to serve (optional)

Mirliton

4 eggs

100 g (3½ oz) sugar

40 g (1½ oz/⅓ cup) icing (confectioner's) sugar

160 g (5⅔ oz) double (thick) cream

80 g (2¾ oz/¾ cup) almond meal (ground almonds)

finely grated zest of 1 lemon

30 g (1 oz) unsalted butter, melted

Shortcrust pastry

120 g (4¼ oz) unsalted butter, softened

80 g (2¾ oz) icing (confectioner's) sugar, sifted

25 g (1 oz/¼ cup) almond meal (ground almonds)

1 teaspoon vanilla extract

2 pinches of salt

1 egg

200 g (7 oz/1⅓ cups) plain (all-purpose) flour

To make the shortcrust pastry, in a bowl, add the butter, icing sugar, almond meal, vanilla extract and salt. Mix with a spatula until all the ingredients are incorporated. Add the egg and mix again. Add the flour and mix without overworking the dough. Wrap the dough and refrigerate for at least 1 hour.

Preheat the oven to 180°C (350°F/Gas 4).

To make the mirliton, in a bowl, break the eggs, add both the sugars, the double cream, almond meal, lemon zest and melted butter. Mix well for 1 minute.

Roll out the dough to about 2 mm (1/16 inch) thick and use to line a 20 cm (8 inch) fluted tart ring (round or square) placed on a baking tray. Cut off the excess dough. Place a mix of frozen berries in the base of the tart and top with the mirliton mixture.

Bake for about 40 minutes, then carefully transfer the tart to a wire rack and cool down completely before removing the ring.

To serve, dust with icing sugar, finish with fresh berries. Serve with a fresh berry coulis and berry sorbet if desired.

Presented in 1997

Liquorice parfait with lime syrup

Serves 6

Place the liquorice and cream into a small saucepan over low heat and heat gently without boiling until the liquorice is soft. Place the mixture in a food processor or blender and blend until smooth. Strain through a fine-mesh sieve, cool, then refrigerate until cold.

In a stainless steel bowl, over a large saucepan of gently simmering water, make a sabayon. This is done by whisking together the eggs, egg yolk, glucose, sugar and Pernod, until the mixture turns pale and fluffy. Remove from the heat and continue whisking until it cools a little.

Fold half of the sabayon into the liquorice mixture. Once combined, fold in the remaining sabayon. Pour into five 125 ml (4 fl oz/½ cup) capacity moulds and freeze.

Meanwhile, to make the lime syrup, using a vegetable peeler, remove the zest in long strips, then juice the lime. Use a small sharp knife to remove any bitter white pith from the zest, then cut into a fine julienne. Place the zest in a small saucepan, cover with water and bring to the boil. Drain and repeat two times.

Place the sugar and the 50 ml of water in a small saucepan and stir over low heat until the sugar dissolves, then bring to the boil. Add the lime juice to taste, then stir in the zest and set aside to cool.

To serve, dip the base of the moulds in hot water for a few seconds, then invert the parfaits onto plates. Scatter a few lime segments around each plate, then drizzle with a little syrup and some of the zest.

50 g (1¾ oz) liquorice

240 ml (8 fl oz) cream

2 eggs

1 egg yolk

12 g (¼ oz) liquid glucose

42 g (1½ oz) caster (superfine) sugar

Pernod, to taste

lime segments, to serve

Lime syrup

1 lime

50 g (1¾ oz) sugar

50 ml (1¾ fl oz) water

Presented in 2003

Caramelised galette of almonds

Serves 6

250 g (9 oz) butter puff pastry

75 g (2⅔ oz) slivered almonds

75 g (2⅔ oz) icing
(confectioner's) sugar

Frangipane

300 g (10½ oz) unsalted butter,
softened

5 eggs

1 teaspoon vanilla essence

300 g (10½ oz) caster
(superfine) sugar

300 g (10½ oz/3 cups) almond meal
(ground almonds)

1 tablespoon Bundaberg Rum OP

Preheat the oven to 180°C (350°F/Gas 4).

To make the frangipane, combine all the ingredients together.

Roll out the puff pastry into a 3 mm (⅛ inch) thick sheet, about
35 cm x 20 cm (14 x 8 inches), place on a baking tray and prick all
over. Spread with the frangipane, leaving a small border, sprinkle with
the slivered almonds, dust generously with the icing sugar and bake for
about 25 minutes or until the icing sugar caramelises and the pastry is
cooked through. It may be necessary to finish the job with a blowtorch.

Antonio Carluccio

Presented in 1999

Fried raviolo with orange blossom honey

Serves 4

4 circles of fresh pecorino cheese, about 10 cm (4 inches) in diameter and 5 mm (¼ inch) thick

olive oil, for deep-frying

80 ml (2½ fl oz/⅓ cup) orange blossom honey, warmed

Dough

300 g (10½ oz/2 cups) plain (all-purpose) flour

2 eggs

2 egg yolks

pinch of salt

2 tablespoons caster (superfine) sugar

To make the dough, pile the flour up into a volcano shape on a work surface and make a large well in the centre. Put the eggs, egg yolk, salt and sugar in the well and beat lightly with a fork. With your hands, gradually mix in the flour. When the mixture has formed a dough, knead it well with the palms of your hands for about 10 minutes or until it is very smooth and elastic. Cover and leave to rest for 20 minutes.

Roll out the dough until it is about 2 mm (¹⁄₁₆ inch) thick. Cut out 8 rounds, each 15 cm (6 inches) in diameter, re-rolling the trimmings as necessary.

Put a piece of pecorino cheese in the centre of 4 of the rounds. Brush the edges of the dough rounds with water and cover with the remaining dough rounds, gently pressing the edges together to seal.

Heat plenty of olive oil in a deep-sided saucepan and fry the ravioli for about 3–4 minutes or until brown and crisp on both sides. Put on individual serving plates, pour the honey over and serve immediately.

Elena Arzak's Hydromel and
Fractal Fluid presented in 2011.

Chapter Three

New Food

Much of the experimentation with food, ingredients and cooking techniques has come out of Spain — San Sebastián in particular — in recent years. There's little surprise, then, that the Melbourne Food and Wine Festival, always interested in the currents and eddies of the greater food world, has featured leading proponents of this new Spanish style like Elena Arzak and Andoni Luis Aduriz. And while their recipes and techniques might be a stretch for the home cook in a domestic kitchen, the challenge of attempting to re-create the magic of these fearsomely talented and intelligent chefs may be hard for some to resist.

But Spain is not the only place in the world pushing boundaries as the roll call at MasterClass has proved. Sat Bains, "the most wildly inventive chef to emerge from Britain since Heston Blumenthal" according to *The Daily Telegraph*, bravely mixes flavours and influences to brilliant effect, while Quay's Peter Gilmore can, through artistic technique make magic out of even the most prosaic ingredients.

Probably the most amazing thing about these new food proponents is that they are still able to surprise and delight us with their take on flavours and textures. And there's nothing quite so satisfying as the shock of the new.

Presented in 2010

Bacon dashi with peas, cucumber, leeks and daikon

Serves 10

2 litres (70 fl oz) bacon dashi

10 raw sugarsnap peas

1 large English cucumber, thinly sliced

3 leeks, thinly sliced and sautéed in oil

1 quick salt-pickled daikon *(see recipe below)*

Bacon dashi

2 pieces konbu (8 cm × 16 cm/ 3¼ × 6¼ inches)

2 litres (70 fl oz) water

250 g (9 oz) piece of smoky bacon

Quick salt-pickled daikon

1 large or 3 small daikon radishes, peeled and cut into very thin slices

1 tablespoon sugar, or more to taste

1 teaspoon kosher or sea salt, or more to taste

Bacon dashi

Rinse the konbu under running water, then combine it with the water in a medium saucepan. Bring the water to a simmer over medium heat and turn off the stove. Leave to steep for 10 minutes.

Remove the konbu from the saucepan and add the bacon. Bring to a boil, then turn the heat down so the water simmers gently. Simmer for 30 minutes.

Strain the bacon from the dashi, and chill the broth until the fat separates and hardens into a solid cap on top of it. Remove and discard the fat and use the dashi or store it. Bacon dashi will keep, covered, for a few days in the refrigerator. Makes 2 litres (70 fl oz).

Quick salt-pickled daikon

Combine the daikon with the sugar and salt in a small mixing bowl and toss to coat. Leave it to sit for 5–10 minutes.

Taste: if the pickles are too sweet or too salty, put them into a colander, rinse off the seasoning, and dry in a tea towel. Taste again and add more sugar or salt as needed. Serve after 5–10 minutes, or refrigerate for up to 4 hours.

To serve

For each serving, pour approximately 200 ml (7 fl oz) of bacon dashi into a bowl or glass. Add a sugarsnap pea and a little of the cucumber, leek and daikon.

From *Momofuku*, David Chang and Peter Meehan, Clarkson Potter (a division of Random House Inc) (2009).

Great diversity. Best Chinese food I've ever had. Best coffee in the world! ...
It's a grown-up slumber party. Lots of fun, well organised and the whole
crew couldn't have been more hospitable. DAVID CHANG, 2010

Peter Gilmore

Presented in 2010

Confit of Suffolk lamb loin, fresh milk curd, asparagus, spring onions, broad beans, young leeks, sunflower seeds, pine nuts, hazelnuts, quinoa, pea flowers, nasturtiums

Serves 8

Artichokes

Artichokes
5 globe artichokes
juice of ½ lemon
100 ml (3½ fl oz) white wine
120 ml (3¾ fl oz) extra virgin olive oil
1 litre (35 fl oz/4 cups) water
½ onion, finely chopped
½ carrot, finely chopped
2 fresh bay leaves
2 sprigs thyme
4 French shallots (eschalots), finely diced
1 stick white celery, finely diced
1 garlic clove, finely diced
500 ml (17 fl oz/2 cups) chicken stock
50 g (1¾ oz) unsalted butter
sea salt

Cook the artichokes by preparing the cooking liquid. Place the lemon juice, wine, 100 ml (3½ fl oz) of the olive oil and the water in a medium saucepan. Add the onion, carrot, bay leaves and thyme and bring the liquid to the boil.

There are two ways you can cook the artichokes. You can peel them and strip back the outside leaves to expose the heart, then poach them in the liquid for 10–15 minutes. You will need to cover the artichokes with silicone paper. Alternatively, you can produce this cooking liquid, using only 250 ml (9 fl oz/1 cup) of water, place it in a vacuum bag with the peeled artichokes, seal the bag and steam it on high for 10–12 minutes.

Once the artichokes are tender, split them in half and remove the choke.

In a clean saucepan, add the remaining olive oil and the finely diced shallots, celery and garlic and sweat gently until the vegetables are softened but don't allow to colour.

Add the cooked artichokes and chicken stock. Simmer for 15 minutes or until almost all the liquid has evaporated.

Place the contents of the saucepan into an upright blender and add the unsalted butter. Blend on high until smooth, pass the purée through a fine sieve, season to taste with sea salt and put aside.

Lamb

Lamb

4 × 8-bone Suffolk lamb racks (with cap on)

Vegetables

16 asparagus spears

4 pods of broad (fava) beans

16 spring onion (scallion) bulbs

16 young leeks

Nuts, seeds and grains

50 g (1¾ oz) hazelnuts

50 g (1¾ oz) sunflower seeds

300 ml (10½ fl oz) clarified butter

50 g (1¾ oz) pine nuts

20 g (¾ oz) puffed quinoa

100 ml (3½ fl oz) brown butter

Fresh milk curd

400 ml (14 fl oz) fresh Jersey cow's milk

10 ml (⅓ fl oz) water

1 ml rennet

continued >

Lamb

Remove and reserve the fat cap. Remove the meat from the bone and completely remove the sinew from the meat. Cut each piece of meat in half to yield 8 equal portions. Place in the refrigerator.

Render down all the fat from the cap of the lamb rack in a small saucepan on a low heat. When the fat is completely melted, pass it through a fine sieve and allow it to cool slightly.

Remove the meat from the refrigerator and coat each piece of meat with the rendered lamb fat. The lamb fat should solidify on the cold meat. Place in Cryovac bags and seal. Refrigerate the lamb until required.

Vegetables

Peel the asparagus and cut the heads off at 4–5 cm (1½–2 inches) in length. Reserve the rest of the asparagus for another use. Pod the broad beans, blanch them in boiling water for 30 seconds, then refresh in iced water and remove the outer shells. Trim and peel the spring onions and leeks. Put aside the vegetables until required.

Nuts, seeds and grains

Preheat the oven to 180°C (350°F/Gas 4). Place the hazelnuts on a baking tray and roast for 10 minutes. Place the hot nuts in a clean tea towel and rub off the papery skins, then cut each nut in half.

Boil the sunflower seeds for 1 minute in boiling water, drain and rub on a tea towel to remove the outer husks.

In a frying pan, melt the clarified butter and separately toast all of the nuts, seeds and puffed quinoa until golden brown. Combine the nuts, seeds and quinoa and dress with the melted brown butter and put aside.

Fresh milk curd

Heat the milk to 40°C (104°F). Mix the water and rennet together. Stir the milk to create a whirlpool in the saucepan and have 8 ceramic dariole moulds ready. Add the water mixture to the swirling milk, then quickly fill the dariole moulds. The milk will only take 1–2 minutes to completely set and it should be stable and remain warm for a good 5–10 minutes in the moulds. Keep the moulds in a warm area.

Melbourne has a vibrant food culture that is self-evident in the general public's enthusiasm for good food and wine. It has a restaurant scene that is keen to push boundaries and develop great concepts. PETER GILMORE, 2010

To serve

50 g (1¾ oz) unsalted butter, melted

sea salt

200 ml (7 fl oz) lamb jus

100 ml (3½ fl oz) pouring (single) cream, whipped

16 nasturtium leaves

16 pea flowers

16 okra shoots

16 rocket (arugula) flowers

8 wild sorrel shoots

To serve

Preheat the oven to 180°C (350°F/Gas 4).

To cook the lamb, prepare a water bath at 68°C (155°F). Submerge the lamb in the water bath and, depending on the thickness of the loins, you will need to cook them for 20–25 minutes to produce an even medium-rare.

In the meantime have a saucepan of salted boiling water ready. Blanch all the vegetables, starting with the spring onions, then the asparagus and leeks. The vegetables will need about 2 minutes. In the last 5 seconds, add the double-shelled broad beans. Drain the vegetables, brush them with melted butter and season with sea salt.

Remove the lamb from the water bath. Cut open the vacuum bags and place the loins on a silicone mat-lined ovenproof tray and season with sea salt. Coat the lamb with the lamb jus and flash in a medium–hot oven for 1 minute.

Reheat the artichoke purée and fold through the whipped cream. Place a small amount of purée in the centre of each plate, place a piece of lamb in the centre of the purée on each plate.

Garnish with the seasoned vegetables. With a round dessert spoon, scoop out each individual milk curd and place on top of the lamb. Sprinkle each curd with the nuts and seeds mixture. Garnish with the nasturtium leaves, pea flowers, okra shoots, rocket flowers and wild sorrel shoots and serve.

Andoni Luis Aduriz

Presented in 2007

Buttery Idiazabal cheese gnocchi
in salted pork bouillion, contrasting leaves

Serves 4

Buttery Idiazabal cheese gnocchi

Cut the cheese into small 1 cm x 1 cm (½ × ½ inch) squares.

Place the cheese with the water in a Thermomix at 55°C (131°F) on speed 5 for a duration of 10 minutes.

Once the time has elapsed, pass the mixture through a fine chinois.

Refrigerate the mix for 6 hours to separate the fat and water from the solid particles through decantation. Strain through a fine sieve again and discard the solids, making sure there are no pieces of fat or solids in the water.

With a ratio of 10 g (¼ oz) of kuzu for every 100 ml (3½ fl oz) of cheese water, place the cheese water and kuzu in a saucepan and season to taste. Cook the mixture very slowly over medium heat, moving with a silicone spatula all the time so that the mixture achieves a level of elasticity.

Buttery Idiazabal cheese gnocchi

100 g (3½ oz) semi-matured hard sheep's milk cheese (idiazabal)

300 ml (10½ fl oz) still mineral water

25 g (1 oz) kuzu (organic Japanese variety)

salt

Once the mixture is cooked and extremely thick like a gum, place into 2 or 3 piping bags. With a bowl filled with ice and water and the nozzle of the piping bag under the water, proceed to pipe the mixture into the water, cutting off with scissors tiny shapes reminiscent of gnocchi.

Set the gnocchi aside sprinkled with a little bit of salty water on a tray covered with plastic wrap.

Pork bouillion

300 g (10½ oz) salted pork bones

40 g (1½ oz) aged salted pork belly fat

500 g (1 lb 2 oz) pork meat, for roasting

300 g (10½ oz) pork tails

40 g (1½ oz) pork fat

1 jamón bone (prosciutto may be used as a substitute)

40 g (1½ oz) carrot

40 g (1½ oz) leek

80 g (2¾ oz) onion

20 g (¾ oz) chickpeas

20 g (¾ oz) potato

3 litres (105 fl oz) water

Contrasting leaves

extra virgin olive oil

8 red shiso leaves

8 Japanese chervil leaves

8 dill sprigs

Pork bouillion

Preheat the oven to 200°C (400°F/Gas 6). Wash the salted pork bones and salted pork belly fat well, removing the excess salt. Place in a large saucepan of boiling water and blanch to remove any rancid flavour that may be present. Refresh. Place the fresh pork meat in the oven to roast to a golden colour.

Once roasted, place all the ingredients in a large stockpot and simmer for 3–5 hours, skimming any impurities as they surface.

Strain through a fine chinois and then through filter paper. Set aside.

To serve

To serve, reheat the tray of gnocchi in an 80°C (175°F/Gas ¼) oven. Reheat the pork bouillon in a saucepan over low heat.

In a hot and concave plate, place pieces of hot gnocchi. Cover with the pork bouillon and carefully display 5 drops of olive oil around the plate. Finish by arranging the contrasting leaves on the surface of the plate.

It's amazing to come to a place as small as Melbourne and have the opportunity to bump into some of the major food figures of the world. I think it's rather amazing to go to Mugaritz and not meet the chef and then to come to Melbourne and meet him here! ROSE GRAY, 2007

Melbourne is the foodiest city in Australia. We are all food-mad, we have the best produce, the best coffee, the best cocktails, the best ethnic eating and the best home cooks ... Every great country has one city that is its foodie heart, its "stomach". In France, it is Lyon, home to the bouchons, women-led bistros. In Italy, it is Bologna, home to pasta, prosciutto, Parmigiano. In Australia, it is Melbourne. JILL DUPLEIX, 2010

Carlo Cracco

Presented in 2009

Risotto with oil of anchovies, lemon and cocoa

Serves 4

50 g (1¾ oz) pure cocoa

pinch of salt

pinch of chilli powder

1 small French shallot (eschalot),
finely chopped

45 g (1⅔ oz) butter

240 g (8¾ oz) carnaroli
del Pavese rice

50 ml (1¾ fl oz) dry white wine

1 litre (35 fl oz/4 cups) hot water

pepper

50 g (1¾ oz) mascarpone

50 g (1¾ oz) anchovy paste

finely grated zest of 1 lemon

Temper the cocoa to 32°C (90°F), spread it on baking paper and add the salt and chilli powder. Allow to dry, then cut with a round shape of 2.5 cm (1 inch) into 4 discs.

In a frying pan over medium heat, sauté the shallot with the butter, add the rice and toast lightly.

Deglaze with the white wine and continue cooking, slowly adding the water. Cook, stirring occasionally, until it has all been absorbed and the rice is cooked. Adjust the salt and pepper.

Take off the heat, and mix in the mascarpone.

Spread the anchovy paste on the bottom of each plate, distribute the lemon zest, pour the risotto over and flatten. Finish with the cocoa disc.

Darren Purchese and Ian Burch

Presented in 2010

Chocolate turrón, salted caramel, almond

Serves 6

Chocolate sponge

Chocolate sponge
50 g (1¾ oz) egg yolk
240 g (8¾ oz) caster (superfine) sugar
250 g (9 oz) whole eggs
110 g (3¾ oz) egg white
190 g (6¾ oz) plain (all-purpose) flour
30 g (1 oz) cocoa powder
30 g (1 oz) cornflour (cornstarch)
15 g (½ oz) unsalted butter, melted and cooled

Chocolate mousse for turrón
700 ml (24 fl oz) thickened (whipping) cream (35% fat)
100 ml (3½ fl oz) full-cream milk (3.5% fat)
60 g (2¼ oz) trimoline
4 vanilla beans, split and seeds scraped

Preheat the oven to 180°C (350°F/Gas 4).

Beat the egg yolk with 190 g (6¾ oz) of the sugar, then gradually add the whole eggs. Whisk until full in volume, then remove ready for the next step.

In a separate bowl, whisk the egg white with the remaining 50 g (1¾ oz) of the sugar to stiff peaks, then gently fold into the sabayon.

Sieve the flour, cocoa powder and cornflour together and gently fold into the mix until it is all incorporated. Fold through the cooled melted butter. Spread the mixture over 2 baking sheets, approximately 30 cm (12 inches) square and bake for 8–10 minutes or until cooked through.

Remove from the oven and leave to cool naturally. Reserve this sponge for the mousse assembly.

Chocolate mousse for turrón

Line two 30 cm (12 inch) square baking tins or mousse rings with silicone paper and then the previously cooked chocolate sponge and set aside.

Heat 150 ml (5 fl oz) of the cream with the milk, trimoline and the vanilla seeds.

Whisk the remaining cream to three-quarter ribbon stage and refrigerate until needed.

300 g (10½ oz) Chocovic Tarakan chocolate (or other dark chocolate with 70–75% cocoa solids)

130 g (4⅔ oz) free-range egg yolk

2 gold-strength gelatine leaves

Chocolate spray mix

500 g (1 lb 2 oz) Chocovic Kendari chocolate (or other dark chocolate with 60% cocoa solids)

250 g (9 oz) Mycryo cocoa butter

continued >

Chop the chocolate into small pieces and place in a large bowl.

Whisk the yolk lightly and pour into the infused cream. Return back to the heat and cook as for custard to 85°C (185°F), then strain over the chocolate.

Place the mixture in a blender along with the soaked and drained gelatine and blend until homogenous and a smooth, shiny cream is formed. Turn the chocolate cream out into a bowl and leave it to cool down to approximately 30–35°C (86–95°F), then gently fold in the whipped cream until you have a shiny mousse. Pour the mousse on top of the sponge in the two prepared tins or rings, level with a spatula and refrigerate until firm.

Turn out the mousse slabs and, using a hot, sharp knife, cut into 60 portions with the dimensions 2 cm x 7.5 cm (¾ × 3 inches). Place the 60 individual portions of mousse into the freezer. Using a melon baller, scoop out a ball of chocolate mousse from one end of each portion of turrón and discard the ball — the cavity will be filled with the salted caramel later. Place the portions of turrón, except 6 servings, back into the freezer (and use as required). Prepare for chocolate spraying.

Chocolate spray mix

Melt the chocolate to 45°C (113°F) and separately melt the cocoa butter to 45–50°C (113–122°F). Combine the two together and strain through a fine chinois. Place the mix into a Wagner 180P paint spray gun and spray the frozen turrón. Place the sprayed items in the fridge to defrost naturally.

Salted caramel

300 ml (10½ fl oz) pouring (single) cream (35% fat)

180 g (6¼ oz) liquid glucose

190 g (6¾ oz) sugar

8 g salt

150 g (5½ oz) unsalted butter

180 ml (5¾ fl oz) milk

Almond cream

150 g (5½ oz) blanched whole almonds

15 g (½ oz) roasted blanched whole almonds

30 g (1 oz) sugar

2 g salt

750 ml (24 fl oz) full-cream milk

70 g (2½ oz) Sosa Gelcrem (modified potato starch)

Dark chocolate and almond aero mix

500 g (1 lb 2 oz) Chocovic Tarakan dark chocolate (75% cocoa solids)

50 g (1¾oz) Mycryo cocoa butter

Sosa almond essence, to taste

To assemble

Golden Murray River salt flakes

Salted caramel

Place the cream into a saucepan and scald.

Place all the other ingredients into an over-sized, heavy-based saucepan and bring to the boil, whisking continuously. Proceed to heat and whisk until 147°C (297°F).

At this point, add the scalded cream and whisk (be careful as the mixture will expand furiously), remove from the heat and cool. Place into a piping bag and reserve at room temperature until ready to use.

Almond cream

Blitz the almonds, sugar, salt and milk in a blender and leave to infuse for a minimum of 8 hours and a maximum of 16 hours. Strain the mix through a muslin cloth (cheesecloth) and place the liquid into a blender. Blend the mix with the Gelcrem for 1 minute on high and reserve in a piping bag until ready to use.

Dark chocolate and almond aero mix

Melt the chocolate and cocoa butter separately to a maximum of 45°C (113°F), then combine the two and add the almond essence to taste. Pour the mixture into a heat-sensitive cream canister. Seal with the lid and charge with four cream-whipping bulbs, vigorously shaking the canister in between each charge. Discharge the mixture into a shallow plastic container and store in the freezer until solid. Break off pieces of the desired shape and size and store in a container at room temperature.

To assemble

Place the sprayed turrón onto each plate and pipe salted caramel into the cavity. Pipe almond cream onto the plate. Sprinkle golden salt onto the caramel and arrange a nice piece of chocolate and almond aero mix on top. Serve.

Every year the Festival seems to get better and better. This is my favourite time of year and it is seen as one of the best organised and most exciting events of its kind in the world. DARREN PURCHESE, 2010

Michael Meredith, Langham
Melbourne MasterClass, 2009.

Tales from MasterClass

MasterClass is the engine under the hood, the nuts and bolts. It's been an integral part of the Melbourne Food and Wine Festival's personality since it was first conceived, creating an up-close and personal arena in which the world's best get to strut their skills, reveal their secrets, their talents, their idiosyncrasies, their personalities and answer questions from a highly informed crowd. It started at the Grand Hyatt, then moved to the Sofitel before moving to the Langham Melbourne hotel, where it's kept under close watch by executive chef Anthony Ross, who re-creates all the tastings at MasterClass. It's live, mostly unscripted with the aromas of the food and the fragrance of the wine reaching the audience in real time. There's certainly room for mistakes but that means there's also plenty of room for magic.

Over the past 20 years, the MasterClass line-up has, to say the least, been starry, featuring more than 20 chefs who bristle with Michelin stars and have held a top place in the S.Pellegrino World's 50 Best Restaurants list. The line-up has included Ferran Adrià, Heston Blumenthal, René Redzepi, Thomas Keller, Andoni Luis Aduriz, Elena Arzak, Massimo Bottura, Inaki Aizpitarte, Alex Atala, Fergus Henderson, Neil Perry, Charlie Trotter, Rose Gray, Michel Roux, Phil Howard, Carlo Cracco, Dieter Mueller, Claude Bosi, David Kinch, David Chang and Peter Gilmore.

The ability of MasterClass to surprise as well as inform started from the beginning when, at the 1993 Festival, Italian-born, US-based chef Giuliano Bugialli was demonstrating how to make pasta when one of the audience members, horrified, shrieked, "But Mr Bugialli, you're using your fingers!" The chef won both applause and approval and set something of an informal benchmark for Melbourne's MasterClass when he good-naturedly but pointedly threw pasta at the woman.

Part of the energy of MasterClass has always come from the fact that chaos is never too far away. Sylvia Johnson remembers a thoroughly

frightened Maggie Beer, "so scared she was almost wobbling" before her first class, who then won the crowd over with her (seemingly) effortless charm; US chef Mark Miller, much delayed due to flight cancellations, arriving in Melbourne only a few hours before he was to present and being confronted by a fully staffed Grand Hyatt kitchen that had completed most of his prep for him; and Trotter, gone AWOL to taste Grange Hermitage in South Australia, flying back just in time to pull an all-nighter and then completely silencing the room when he gave them a taste of his exquisite "tomato water".

In more recent times there has been the sight of chef Ben Shewry, sitting in on Korean-American Roy Choi's class, putting up his hand to ask for the secret to a successful tortilla (the juice of one lime apparently) and Hong Kong chef Margaret Xu teaching the team from Melbourne's Ezard restaurant how to make tofu from scratch in exchange for them teaching her how to make chlorophyll. Nigella Lawson won the crowd over with her passion for home cooking while Michelin-starred Atul Kochhar did the same with his detailed descriptions and demonstrations of roasting spices.

Heston Blumenthal, writing in *Australian Gourmet Traveller* about his experience at the 2009 Festival said, "What I really liked about the MasterClasses was that they were kept small. Some of the big European festivals are more like trade conventions. There's also a real mix of amateurs and professionals in the room. We had a book signing afterwards; signed a few body parts as well and there was one bloke who said he was too tight to buy a book so I signed his train ticket instead."

Expert cooking, signed body parts, organised chaos — all in a day's work at MasterClass.

What I liked about [Langham Melbourne MasterClass] ... was that there was a real mix of amateurs and professionals in the room and gauging by the questions asked everyone seemed really interested.

HESTON BLUMENTHAL, 2009

Clockwise from top left: Zakary Pelaccio, Langham Melbourne MasterClass, 2011; Nigella Lawson, Theatre of Ideas 2011; George Calombaris, Langham MasterClass, 2011; Alla Wolf-Tasker, Langham Melbourne MasterClass, 2011; Rachel Allen, Langham Melbourne MasterClass, 2011 Michael Psilakis, Langham Melbourne MasterClass, 2010.

Elena Arzak

Presented in 2011

Hydromel and fractal fluid

Serves 4

For the "broken" base

250 g (9 oz/1⅔ cups) plain (all-purpose) flour

125 g (4½ oz) unsalted butter, chopped

1 whole egg

1 egg yolk

1 tablespoon water

100 g (3½ oz) sugar

1.5 g tandoori spice

1.5 g sweet paprika

0.5 g cochineal (carmine dye)

20 g (¾ oz) blue curaçao

10 g (¼ oz) apple liqueur

For the lemon sculptures

150 g (5½ oz) lemon juice

2 lemons, zest removed in wide strips

2 whole eggs

2 egg yolks

100 g (3½ oz) unsalted butter

50 g (1¾ oz) liquid glucose

50 g (1¾ oz) milk

For the "broken" base

Combine all the ingredients, except the blue curaçao and apple liqueur, together until a dough forms, cover in plastic wrap and refrigerate for 1 hour.

Preheat the oven to 140˚C (275˚F/Gas 1).

Extend the mixture over a baking tray and bake for 1 hour 20 minutes. Cool, then break into small pieces.

Pour the curaçao and apple liqueur over 150 g (5½ oz) of the broken base.

For the lemon sculptures

Place all the ingredients in a saucepan and stir to combine well. Bring to the boil, then remove the lemon zest. Pour into four flexible square moulds, about 3 cm (1¼ inch) square. Place in the freezer. Once hard, cut them in half and roll into balls. Return to the freezer.

For outside of the lemon sculptures

200 g (7 oz) cocoa butter

3 g sweet paprika

0.5 g cochineal (carmine dye)

For the hydromel base

500 g (17 oz/2 cups) water

100 g (3½ oz) honey

2 star anise

100 g (3½ oz) birch sugar

1.5 g xanthan gum

For the hydromel reaction

10 g (¼ oz) vodka

1.7 g cochineal (carmine dye)

1 teaspoon water

2 g sugar

For the final step and presentation

extra-bitter cocoa powder, for dusting

For outside of the lemon sculptures

Melt the cocoa butter, making sure the temperature does not exceed 50˚C (122˚F). Mix in the paprika and cochineal. Using a hypodermic needle, bathe the frozen lemon sculptures with this mixture, just enough so that it creates a film over the exterior. Leave to stand in the fridge.

For the hydromel base

Boil the water and honey together. Once boiling, add the star anise, remove from the heat and leave to infuse for 5 minutes, then remove the star anise. Leave to cool.

Add the rest of the ingredients, mixing well with the help of an electric mixer. Place in the fridge and leave for 6 hours to allow the air in the mixture to dissipate.

For the hydromel reaction

Mix all the ingredients and pour into a jug.

For the final step and presentation

Dust the "sculptures" with the cocoa powder until they become a dark brown.

On a flat plate or black board, place the "broken base", then the sculptures standing up (2 per person).

Pour 50 g (1¾ oz) of the hydromel base onto a plate. When the waiter/ess takes the dish to the table, he/she will pour the hydromel reactive mixture over the top, using a teaspoon to produce a fractal reaction.

My Last Supper — The Dinner,
Meat Market, North Melbourne, 2008.

Roy Choi, Coda Restaurant, 2011.

Frank Camorra

Presented in 2009

Pan con chocolate

(Chocolate with bread)

Serves 6

Gently melt the chocolate in a bowl placed over a saucepan of simmering water for 5 minutes, stirring occasionally. Ensure the base of the bowl doesn't touch the water.

Remove from the heat, whisk in the egg yolks, then the butter and stir until all the butter has melted.

In another bowl, whisk the egg white until soft peaks form, then, whisking continuously, gradually add the sugar. Do not overbeat.

Mix one-third of the meringue into the chocolate mixture until nearly combined, then gently fold through the remaining meringue.

300 g (10½ oz) dark chocolate (50% cocoa solids), chopped

4 eggs, separated

100 g (3½ oz) unsalted butter, softened

2 tablespoons caster (superfine) sugar

200 g (7 oz) firm two-day old white bread (high-tin loaf), crusts removed and cut into 2 mm (¹⁄₁₆ inch) thick slices, then into 8 cm × 2 cm (3¼ × ¾ inch) fingers

olive oil (Hojiblanca brand), to drizzle

good-quality sea salt flakes, to sprinkle

Pour the mixture into a greased and baking paper-lined 25 cm × 10 cm (10 × 4 inch) loaf tin, cover and refrigerate for 1 hour or until just set.

It should be served not too cold and just set, so it is important to make this very close to the time required.

Meanwhile, preheat the oven to 180°C (350°F/Gas 4).

Place the bread slices in a single layer on a baking tray, then cover with another baking tray the same size and bake for 15 minutes or until crisp. Cool, then place the wafers in an airtight container.

To serve, invert the chocolate onto a chopping board and cut into slices. Drizzle with olive oil, then sprinkle with a tiny pinch of salt. Serve with the bread wafers.

Sat Bains

Presented in 2009

Chocolate cream, rapeseed oil, toast, sea salt

Serves 6

Chocolate cream

250 g (9 oz) milk

250 g (9 oz) pouring (single) cream

100 g (3½ oz) egg yolk

250 g (9 oz) chocolate
(70% cocoa solids), chopped

Rapeseed oil jelly

200 g (7 oz) water

50 g (1¾ oz) sugar

50 g (1¾ oz) liquid glucose

50 g (1¾ oz) isomalt

2 leaves bronze-strength
gelatine, soaked in iced water
for 10 minutes, then drained and
excess water squeezed out

160 g (5⅔ oz) rapeseed oil

Sweet toast

½ loaf good-quality white
sourdough baguette

olive oil, for drizzling

sea salt and sugar, for sprinkling

Chocolate cream

Whisk together the milk, cream and egg yolk and heat up to 86°C (187°F). Pour over the chocolate and emulsify. Leave to cool.

Rapeseed oil jelly

Bring the water, sugar, glucose and isomalt to a boil, remove from the heat, then stir in the gelatine until dissolved. Whisking continuously, gradually add the oil until emulsified. Pour into a container, cool, then refrigerate until set.

Sweet toast

Preheat the oven to 160°C (315°F/Gas 2–3). Slice the baguette as thinly as possible. Drizzle with a little olive oil and sprinkle over some salt and sugar. Bake until golden brown.

Caramelised rice krispies

300 g (10½ oz) water

600 g (1 lb 5 oz) sugar

300 g (10½ oz) rice krispies

120 g (4¼ oz) unsalted butter

Aerated chocolate

500 g (1 lb 2 oz) milk chocolate

75 g (2⅔ oz) groundnut oil

400 g (14 oz) caramelised rice krispies *(see recipe above)*

To assemble

sugar, for coating

sea salt, for sprinkling

Caramelised rice krispies

Bring the water and sugar up to the boil. When the sugar starts to caramelise, add the rice krispies and stir to coat in the caramel. Add the butter to stop them sticking together and place onto a tray lined with silicone paper.

Aerated chocolate

Melt the chocolate and the oil until 42°C (108°F), place in a heat-sensitive cream canister and charge with three bulbs. Line a deep tray with silicone paper, then the rice krispies. Pipe the contents of the canister out over the rice krispies and leave to set.

To assemble

Place a quenelle of the chocolate cream off centre in a bowl. Take a teaspoon of the rapeseed oil jelly and roll it in a little sugar. Place it next to the quenelle. Sprinkle a few grains of sea salt over the chocolate cream, crumble over a little of the aerated chocolate and finish with a piece of the sweet toast.

Melbourne Food and Wine Festival has long been considered a ritual on the international calendar — a chance to meet, share ideas, experiment with flavours and get inspired. It is a high-voltage cultural experience. GUY GROSSI, 2010

Sam Bompas & Harry Parr, presenting alongside
Ian Burch and Darren Purchese, Theatre of Ideas, 2011.

Collaborations

Part of the reason for the success and the rigour of the Melbourne Food and Wine Festival is that it receives so much support from the industry. A large part of this support comes from the fact that the local winemakers and chefs get to meet, learn from, exchange ideas with, even teach a thing or two, to their visiting colleagues. And with a roll call of visitors that seems to keep getting starrier (the 2010 contingent of visiting chefs brought, combined, more than 20 Michelin stars with them) there's a huge opportunity for the exchange of knowledge, the making of friendships and some pretty interesting collaborations.

The collaborations are often memorable. There's the sight of Momofuku's David Chang creating his take on modern Korean food alongside Andrew McConnell at the open kitchen of Cumulus Inc., a synthesis that may not have looked so probable on paper but was palpable between the chefs and triumphantly expressed on the plate.

Raymond Capaldi teamed up with René Redzepi to create a dinner, part of which involved the chefs going out to look for rocks which would be used to plate up one of René's signature mollusc dishes. Capaldi identified the Ivanhoe golf course as a good source of such rocks but while they were loading them into the car they had a close encounter with several large and slightly menacing kangaroos, something the Noma chef had not experienced in any of his previous foraging experiences.

Then there was the obvious bonding of like minds between Attica's Ben Shewry and Danish chef Thorsten Schmidt who spent time on the Bellarine Peninsula foraging for the food that they would later cook together at a Festival dinner, or the moment between Spain's Elena Arzak and Vue de Monde's Shannon Bennett when they compared notes on the trials of getting their young children to eat their food.

It's the performance art of MoVida, Melbourne's most famous Spanish restaurant, giving its kitchens over to London's Thomasina Miers so

she could turn the tapas bar into a Mexican restaurant for a night, or the amazing magic when the Royal Mail's Dan Hunter teamed up with his former boss, Andoni Luis Aduriz from Mugaritz to create, among a list of incredible concoctions, an edible soap, complete with honey bubbles that was, according to Aduriz, his way at getting back at the cosmetic industry who are increasingly using edible ingredients in their products.

It's the sight of LA taco truck maestro Roy Choi mixing cocktails behind the bar at Gerald's; Mark Miller and Madhur Jaffrey "getting stuck into an incredibly intellectual argument about third-century artifacts or something" at the Flower Drum; Antonio Carluccio and Michel Roux debating over lunch whether French or Italian cuisine was the superior; pastry makers Ian Burch and Darren Purchese making salted caramel in the shape of gold bullion for Nigella Lawson; and Tasmanian preserving queen Sally Wise passing her tried and true hangover cure to London's jellymongers, Bompas & Parr. The spirit of collaboration, it seems, is part of what gives the Festival its beating heart.

The space where the demonstration was held was spectacular ... the demonstrations from the other chefs were very interesting, and the number of people attending really surprised us all; maybe because we are used to having an audience mainly comprised of cooks, critics and restaurant people, but here we saw well-rounded audience.

ANDONI LUIZ ADURIZ, 2010

Clockwise from top left: Kylie Kwong and Karen Martini, Delicious Double Acts, 2003; Stephanie Alxander and Maggie Beer, Delicious Double Acts, 2004; Christine Manfield and Geoff Lindsay, Delicious Double Acts, 2003; Valli Little and Matt Moran, 2003; Bill Granger and Jill Dupleix, 2003; Alastair McLeod and Anna Gare, Theatre of Ideas, 2011.

Presented in 2010

King prawn, potato, passionfruit and sage

Serves 4

Dice the potato into 5 mm (¼ inch) cubes. Simmer in the dashi stock and butter until just tender, then drain, reserving both the liquid and the potato. Reduce the cooking liquid down to a glaze. Add the potatoes back to the pan and toss through the glaze.

Scoop out the pulp from the passionfruit. Set aside.

Chiffonade the sage. Set aside.

1 desiree potato
200 ml (7 fl oz) dashi stock
25 g (1 oz) butter, plus extra for cooking
1 passionfruit
1 bunch sage, leaves picked
olive oil, for cooking
4 extra large king prawns (shrimp), peeled and deveined
extra dashi stock, for glazing

Pan-fry the prawns gently in butter and olive oil in a non-stick frying pan until just warm in the centre (about 30–60 seconds either side). Remove from the pan and set aside.

Deglaze the frying pan with the extra dashi stock and reduce to a glaze.

Fold the sage through the potatoes.

To assemble

Arrange some of the glazed potato onto a plate. Place a prawn on the side and spoon over a small amount of the passionfruit pulp. Spoon over the glaze from the pan.

David Chang, Langham
MasterClass, 2010.

Stars of Spice,
The Gala Dinner, 2011.

Chapter four

Spice Stars

At 2011's Melbourne Food and Wine Festival, Atul Kochhar, the first Indian chef to score a Michelin star, was on the MasterClass stage individually roasting a whole variety of spices that were to go into his dish, a Goa-style roast poussin. It was important, he noted, not to roast the spices together as they all had their different roasting times and distinct aromas and should be kept separate until the cooking is under way. The theory could also apply to the line-up of spice-driven chefs who have joined the MasterClass roll call over the years. They're brilliant individual chefs who come together for the Festival to create a totally satisfying blend. These people include: Neil Perry, a proven master of spice in many different cuisines; Elizabeth Chong, the Melbourne Food and Wine Festival Legend, who has done so much to bring authenticity and respect to Chinese cuisine; and Tony Tan, whose cooking school has been praised as one of the best in the world. Together, the recipes of these spice aficionados demonstrate just how versatile and ethereally beautiful these flavours and aromas can be.

Third from left: Atul Kochhar, 2011; *fifth from left:* Elizabeth Chong, cooking in the Myer windows, 2007.

David Thompson

Presented in 2000

Prawn and pomelo on betel leaves

Makes 8

20 g (¾ oz) roasted grated coconut

10 g (¼ oz) roasted peanuts

10 g (¼ oz) dried prawns (shrimp)

1 slice roasted galangal

1 Thai bird's eye chilli (scuds)

pinch of salt

100 g (3½ oz) palm sugar (jaggery)

50 ml (1¾ fl oz) water

30 ml (1 fl oz) fish sauce

30 ml (1 fl oz) tamarind water

20 g (¾ oz) extra roasted grated coconut

10 g (¼ oz) young ginger, cubed

30 g (1 oz) red Asian shallots, cubed

1 slice of lime, finely cubed

squeeze of lime juice

30 g (1 oz) pomelo flesh

4 blanched prawns, sliced

coriander (cilantro) leaves

8 betel leaves

Using a pestle and mortar, pound the coconut with the peanuts, dried prawns, galangal, chilli and salt until quite fine.

Heat the palm sugar with the water. When dissolved, add the coconut paste and simmer for several minutes until the syrup is quite thick. Add the fish sauce and continue to simmer until you can smell the galangal, then add the tamarind water. Do not simmer for too long after the tamarind has been added or it will become scorched. Do not reduce too much or when the dressing has cooled it will be too hard. Remove from the heat. Cool.

Combine the remaining ingredients except the betel leaves. Dress with the sauce and serve on the betel leaves.

Presented in 1997

Deep-fried prawn dumplings with tomato and ginger salsa

Makes 60 pieces

Prawn filling

1 tablespoon cooking oil

5 g (⅛ oz) finely minced ginger

150 g (5¼ oz) pork fat, cut into
2 cm × 2 mm (¾ × ¹⁄₁₆ inch) slivers

150 g (5½ oz) bamboo shoots,
finely shredded

75 g (2⅔ oz) fresh shiitake
mushrooms, finely shredded

1 kg (2 lb 4 oz) peeled green
prawns (shrimp), diced or
halved if they are small

20 g (¾ oz) salt

40 g (1½ oz) sugar

40 g (1½ oz) tapioca flour,
combined with 2 tablespoons
water until smooth

10 g (¼ oz) finely chopped white
part of spring onion (scallion)

10 g (¼ oz) finely chopped
coriander (cilantro)

finely ground white pepper, to taste

To make the prawn filling, heat the cooking oil in a wok over medium heat. Add the ginger, pork fat, bamboo shoots and mushrooms and cook for 2 minutes. Add the prawns and cook until the meat turns pink. Add the salt, sugar and tapioca mixture and stir until the prawns are coated with the sauce. Stir in the spring onion, coriander and white pepper, then remove from the heat and cool.

Tomato and ginger salsa

250 g (9 oz) tomato concasse

100 g (3½ oz) finely diced red
onion

20 g (¾ oz) chiffonade of pickled
ginger

10 mint leaves, chiffonade

6 basil leaves, chiffonade

80 ml (2½ fl oz/⅓ cup) Chinese
red vinegar

2 tablespoons balsamic vinegar

125 ml (4 fl oz/½ cup) virgin olive
oil

Pastry

250 ml (9 fl oz/1 cup) boiling water

450 g (1 lb) wheat starch

20 g (¾ oz) melted chicken fat
or lard

To serve

vegetable oil, for deep-frying

rocket (arugula) leaves, to serve

To make the tomato and ginger salsa, combine all the ingredients and set aside until serving.

To make the pastry, pour the boiling water over the wheat starch and stir until clear. Add the chicken fat or lard and knead until a smooth dough forms. Roll out the pastry to 3 mm (⅛ inch) thick sheets and cut into discs using a 10 cm (4 inch) ring cutter.

Spoon a little less than 1 tablespoon of the filling into the middle of each pastry disc, then fold over and just press to seal the edges.

Deep-fry the dumplings very quickly in hot oil, then drain on paper towel. Serve with the salsa and rocket leaves.

Elizabeth Chong

Presented in 1997

Stir-fried beef and bitter melon in black bean sauce

Serves 4 as part of a shared meal

1 tablespoon fermented black beans

½ teaspoon sugar

pinch of salt

2 garlic cloves, bruised

light soy sauce, for drizzling

2 bitter melons

2 tablespoons peanut oil

300 g (10½ oz) rump or fillet steak, sliced and marinated in a light splash of soy sauce, rice wine and a light dusting of potato flour or cornflour (cornstarch)

1 tablespoon chicken stock or water

Rinse the black beans under cold water and drain. Mix in a small bowl with the sugar, salt, garlic and a splash of light soy sauce.

Cut each bitter melon in half lengthways. Scoop out the seeds and surrounding pulp. Cut the melon, across, into 1 cm (½ inch) thick slices.

Bring some water (enough to cover the melon) to a rolling boil, and blanch the melon for 1–2 minutes or until they are slightly softened and become a brighter green. Rinse immediately and briefly under cold running water, then drain and put aside.

Heat a wok over high heat until very hot, add the oil and coat the surface of the wok.

Add the beef slices, stir-frying until the colour changes. Add the black bean mixture, stirring constantly until fragrant.

Add the bitter melon, combining carefully and quickly for the flavours to marry.

Add the chicken stock or water in a thin drizzle, stir-frying to combine all the seasonings evenly. Serve immediately.

Stars of Spice, The Gala Dinner, 2011.

Salt and sugar–cured duck breast
with Sichuan pepper, poached pear and turnip

Serves 4

25 ml (¾ fl oz) cabernet sauvignon vinegar

25 ml (¾ fl oz) olive oil

1 turnip, peeled and thinly sliced into half-moon shapes

150 g (5½ oz) watercress or daikon sprouts, to serve

Duck

50 g (1¾ oz) Sichuan peppercorns, plus extra, ground, for seasoning

60 g (2¼ oz) soft brown sugar

60 g (2¼ oz) rock salt

2 small to medium duck breasts (about 180 g/6¼ oz each)

Poached pears

5 corella pears, peeled and quartered

650 ml (22½ fl oz) sugar syrup

2 star anise, toasted and crushed

½ vanilla bean, split and seeds scraped

1 cinnamon stick

To make the poached pears, place the pear quarters in a saucepan, cover with the syrup and add the star anise, vanilla bean and seeds and cinnamon and bring to a simmer. When the pears are just cooked but firm, take off the stove and allow to cool down in their syrup. These can be stored in the fridge for up to 2 weeks in a sealable jar and are a great accompaniment to yoghurts and breakfast cereals.

To cure the duck, combine the Sichuan peppercorns, brown sugar and rock salt in a non-reactive bowl. Add the duck breasts and cover in the curing mixture. Refrigerate for 2 hours, then rinse the breasts well and pat dry on paper towel.

To make the dressing, process 4 of the poached pear quarters, the vinegar and olive oil in a blender until smooth. Strain through a fine sieve, then season with salt, black pepper and Sichuan pepper to taste.

Core and thinly slice the remaining poached pears.

Preheat the oven to 220°C (425°F/Gas 7). Season the duck breast skin and place, skin side down, in a cold heavy-based frying pan over medium heat and cook for 8–10 minutes. This helps to crisp the skin. Once the skin has rendered enough, place on a baking tray, skin side up, and bake for 2–3 minutes. Take out of the oven and place, skin side down, until needed.

To serve, cook the turnip slices in lightly salted boiling water for 2 minutes, then drain. Toss gently with the poached pear slices and season to taste.

Divide the turnip and pear mixture among serving plates and spoon over a little dressing. Slice the duck (approximately 4 slices per breast) and fan beside the salad. Garnish with watercress or daikon sprouts and drizzle the remaining dressing over and around the dish.

126 Cooking with the World's Best

Teage Ezard

Presented in 1997

Pan-fried Emu Creek sheep's feta with rocket, pear crackers, pomegranate molasses and spicy sugar

Serves 4

1 william pear

400 g (14 oz) square block of sheep's feta

300 ml (10½ fl oz) milk

3 eggs

100 g (3½ oz/⅔ cup) plain (all-purpose) flour

200 g (7 oz) fine breadcrumbs

clarified butter or ghee, for cooking

120 g (4¼ oz) rocket (arugula) leaves

Dressing

100 ml (3½ fl oz) pomegranate molasses

100 ml (3½ fl oz) extra virgin olive oil

pinch of freshly ground black pepper

Spicy sugar

1 tablespoon pure icing (confectioner's) sugar

2 teaspoons ground cinnamon

½ teaspoon allspice

Preheat the oven to 120°C (235°F/Gas ½). Thinly slice the pear and place on a lightly greased wire rack or baking tray and bake until brown and crisp.

To make the dressing, combine all the ingredients in a small bowl.

To make the spicy sugar, sift all the ingredients together and set aside until ready to serve.

Cut the feta into bite-sized triangles, making sure that they are not too thick. Whisk the milk and eggs to form an eggwash. Dust the feta individually in the flour, dip in the eggwash and then in the breadcrumbs.

To serve, pan-fry the feta in clarified butter or ghee over medium heat until golden brown. Drain on paper towel, then place upon the rocket leaves. Drizzle with the dressing. Dust the pear crackers and feta with the sifted spicy sugar and serve.

Neil Perry

Presented in 2005

Steamed snapper fillets with Moroccan flavours

Serves 4

4 × 180 g (6¼ oz) snapper fillets, skin on

1 preserved lemon

½ cup chermoula paste

250 ml (9 fl oz/1 cup) warm water

juice of 1 lemon

sea salt

2 tablespoons honey

2 tablespoons coriander (cilantro) leaves, chopped

Cut the preserved lemon into quarters and remove all the pith with a sharp knife. Cut the rind into thin strips. Set aside.

In a stainless steel bowl, mix the chermoula paste gently with the fish pieces and allow to marinate for 1 hour.

Place the fish in a wide ceramic bowl to steam — a pasta bowl is often a good size for this job. Mix the water, lemon juice, sea salt and honey in the stainless steel bowl with any chermoula that is left in there and pour over the fish. Top with the preserved lemon. Place the bowl in a steamer and steam for about 10–12 minutes — this may vary depending on the bowl you cook the fish in so test gently before removing from the steamer.

To serve, carefully remove each portion of fish with a fish lifter and place in white bowls. Spoon the sauce from the steamer bowl over the fish, sprinkle with the coriander and serve immediately.

This is great served with couscous and a little steamed broccolini with garlic and chilli. If you like it really hot, add a dollop of harissa to the side.

Presented in 2011

Goa-style roasted poussins with coconut gravy and lentil salad

Serves 4

Spice powder

5 cm (2 inch) piece of cinnamon stick

4 whole cloves

3 teaspoons coriander seeds

1 peppercorn

seeds from 10 green cardamom pods

1 star anise

pinch of freshly grated nutmeg

pinch of ground mace

Poussins

4 small lemons, pricked with a fork and softened by rolling with your hands

4 poussins (spatchcocks)

80 ml (2½ fl oz/⅓ cup) vegetable oil

Preheat the oven to 200°C (400°F/Gas 6).

To make the spice powder, place all the whole spices in a dry frying pan over heat and shake until lightly toasted and fragrant. Cool, then finely grind in a spice grinder. Combine in a small bowl with the remaining spices.

Insert the lemons into the poussin cavities and place in a lightly greased roasting tray. Rub each one with oil, then season to taste and sprinkle with 1 teaspoon of the spice mixture. Roast for 20–25 minutes or until just cooked. Remove and rest on a wire rack.

To make the gravy, heat the oil in a heavy-based saucepan over medium heat and sauté the onion till light golden in colour. Add the browned chicken bones, followed by the desiccated coconut. Add the remaining spice powder and cook for 1 minute, then add the chicken stock and bring to the boil. Reduce the heat to low and simmer until reduced by half, then strain and return to the pan. Add the coconut milk to lighten the sauce, then simmer until slightly thickened. Correct the seasoning.

To make the lentil salad, toss all the ingredients together, then serve immediately with the roasted poussins and gravy.

Gravy

2 tablespoons vegetable oil

1 onion, sliced

1 kg (2 lb 4 oz) chicken bones, cooked to brown colour in the oven

45 g (1⅔ oz/½ cup) desiccated coconut, lightly toasted

600 ml (21 fl oz) chicken stock

300 ml (10½ fl oz) coconut milk

Lentil salad

200 g (7 oz) black chickpeas, soaked overnight, then boiled until tender

100 g (3½ oz) green lentils, boiled until *al dente*

1 small bunch watercress, sprigs picked or 1 gem lettuce, leaves separated

1 tomato, diced

1 small red onion, chopped

1 cucumber, diced

1 tablespoon chopped coriander (cilantro)

½ teaspoon finely chopped ginger

1 tablespoon vegetable oil

1 tablespoon lime juice

salt, to taste

1 green chilli, finely chopped (optional)

½ teaspoon cumin seeds, toasted and ground

Melbourne food festival has a very unique energy. Apart from the setting of course, the audience are brilliant, they really want to learn and to know about cooking. It's a really fun event to do.

HESTON BLUMENTHAL, 2009

David Thompson

Presented in 2003

Mixed vegetable and fruit salad dressed with tamarind, palm sugar and sesame seeds

Serves 2

2 handfuls of mixed mint, dill and Thai and lemon basil leaves

1 tablespoon each of grated fresh wasabi and sliced small plantain (optional)

2 tablespoons sliced yam bean (jicama)

2 tablespoons sliced green beans

1 tablespoon shredded pak chi farang (long-leaf coriander)

½ small green mango, shredded

5 cape gooseberries, chopped

2 lemongrass stalks, thinly sliced

1 apple eggplant (aubergine), sliced

4 kaffir lime leaves, shredded

½ star fruit, elegantly sliced

½ small witlof (chicory/Belgian endive), shredded

3 deep-fried long red chillies, roughly crumbled or sliced

Dressing

2 tablespoons palm sugar (jaggery)

125 ml (4 fl oz/½ cup) thick tamarind water

1 tablespoon light soy sauce

1 teaspoon white sesame seeds

2 tablespoons fried red shallots

To make the dressing, melt the palm sugar (if the palm sugar does not have a prime oily quality, then add 1 tablespoon of thick coconut cream). Add the tamarind water and light soy sauce. Toast the sesame seeds until fragrant and golden, then allow to cool. Crush the sesame seeds using a mortar and pestle and stir into the sauce. It should taste sweet, sour and only very slightly salty. Just before serving, stir in the fried red shallots.

Combine the herbs, prepared fruits and vegetables in a bowl. While not every suggested vegetable is necessary, a good selection gives a rounded balance to the salad. Dress and serve.

The Art of Food

As well as being fanatical about food and wine, Melbourne is a town that also prides itself on its cerebral side. Little wonder then that many of the Melbourne Food and Wine Festival programs are dotted with events that link food with art and philosophy. There have been film festivals, art exhibitions, theatre and music performances, debates, forums, even circus acts that have helped people explore further the notions of how, what and where we eat and why we eat the way that we do.

Art made its way into the program four years into the Festival's life with a photographic exhibition, at RMIT's Storey Hall in 1997, that explored the changing face of food photography over the years and highlighted, through a series of historical and current photos of food, the fact that the food industry is as susceptible to the whims of fashion and fad as the rag trade.

Victoria's regional galleries also took to the art–food link, staging a series of dinners inspired by a painting in their permanent collections, while in 2010 several of Melbourne's rooftop bars in the CBD were turned into impromptu gallery spaces, showing works by local artists that not only "responded to the unique flavour of some of our best-loved rooftops" but created the perfect excuse for a bar crawl.

Film has played a fairly constant part in the Festival with food-themed films, ranging from *Breakfast at Tiffany's*, *Willy Wonka & the Chocolate Factory* and *My Dinner with André* to documentaries on everything from the global coffee industry (*Black Gold*) to the daily struggles of strawberry farmers in the north of the Gaza Strip whose crop has to be exported to the rest of the world via military-controlled checkpoints (*Strawberry Fields*). The films are often linked to cooking demonstrations and even dinners, as with the one at Grossi Florentino that used *Like Water For Chocolate* for inspiration.

Melbourne's trams have been used in a variety of forms for the Festival, most notably when the City Circle tram was turned into the Tasting Tram with passengers being offered a variety of bite-sized snacks to go with their journey — the award for the most exuberant use of the tram was in 2002 when the Food Tram transformed a regular trundler into a circus-inspired version of a restaurant kitchen complete with food smells, pyrotechnics and physical theatre.

There's always been plenty of talking and philosophising about food in Melbourne too. In 1998, the Prahran Market was the venue for a Food and Wine Writers' Forum where topics up for discussion ranged from "Is food the opiate of the masses?" to "Do we get the critics we deserve?". In 2008, a whole weekend in Federation Square was devoted to the discussion of all things to do with Slow Food — from cooking and sourcing sustainable seafood to threats to the food supply and the threat of corporate agriculture.

But it has been in more recent times, with the advent of the Theatre of Ideas as part of the MasterClass weekend, that the meaty, thought-provoking discussion of food has found a permanent Festival perch. In *Australian Gourmet Traveller*'s wrap-up of the 2010 Festival, the Theatre of Ideas session with Massimo Bottura from Osteria Francescana in Modena was deemed to be one of that year's highlights: "But it was Massimo Bottura who everyone was talking about as they left the MasterClasses and the Theatre of Ideas. Bottura talked about jazz and rock 'n' roll, Joseph Beuys and Mick Jagger in the same breath as balsamic vinegar and Parmigiano-Reggiano, and it became clear why he has come to be regarded as a compelling (and in some quarters controversial) figure. His Magnum ice cream of foie gras parfait covered in Piedmontese hazelnuts and Sicilian almonds contained a liquid centre of balsamico so ancient it was syrup-like. And then, on the spur of the moment, he made a go-Aussie green-and-gold saffron and asparagus risotto, cheering the crowd as he bubbled over with that most vital quality in a chef, however artistic and cerebral: the overwhelming desire to feed people."

Other names to grace the Theatre of Ideas have been Nigella Lawson, extolling the virtues of great home cooking, Andoni Luis Aduriz explaining why diners are given two cards at the beginning of their meal at his restaurant Mugaritz inviting them to "Submit" or "Rebel" and crazy jellymongers Bompas & Parr discussing why they've taken jelly to new architectural heights and turned food into a performance piece. At Festival time it's as much about the idea and the art of eating as the eating itself.

Clockwise from top left: My Last Supper — The Dinner, Meat Market, North Melbourne, 2008; Jacques Reymond (top right); Alla Wolf-Tasker (bottom centre); Shannon Bennett (bottom left), (three chef portraits by Melanie Dunea for the My Last Supper Exhibition, 2008).

Neil Perry

Presented in 2005

Moroccan-style eggplant salad

Serves 4

2 large eggplants (aubergines),
cut into 1 cm (½ inch) thick slices

sea salt

olive oil, for cooking

½ cup flat-leaf (Italian) parsley
leaves

4 garlic cloves, roughly chopped

3 tomatoes, blanched, peeled,
deseeded and chopped into 8

1 teaspoon ground cumin

extra virgin olive oil

juice of 1 lemon

Salt the eggplant slices well for 1 hour. Wash and pat dry. Heat some olive oil in a frying pan and shallow-fry the eggplant slices, in batches, to a dark golden brown (not black). Remove and drain on paper towel, leaving the oil in the pan.

Add the parsley leaves to the pan and fry quickly. Add the garlic, tomato and cumin and return the eggplant slices to the pan.

Reduce the heat, add a dash of extra virgin olive oil and the lemon juice and mix it all together, breaking the eggplant up well.

Shanghai cabbage or baby bok choy with shiitake mushrooms

Serves 4 as part of a shared meal

1 bunch Shanghai cabbage or baby bok choy (pak choy)

60 ml (2 fl oz/¼ cup) peanut oil

1 teaspoon finely minced ginger

½ teaspoon finely minced garlic

1 tablespoon oyster sauce

3 teaspoons potato flour mixed with 200 ml (7 fl oz) water or chicken stock for thickening

1 teaspoon salt

pinch of sugar

dash of rice wine

Marinated shiitake

10–12 best-quality dried shiitake (Chinese) mushrooms

1 tablespoon dark soy sauce

1 tablespoon light soy sauce

2 teaspoons sugar

½ teaspoon salt

2 teaspoons sesame oil

To make the marinated shiitake, soak the shiitake mushrooms for 30 minutes in warm water, cut off the stems, rinse and squeeze out the excess water. Mix the remaining ingredients together and soak the mushrooms in the marinade for 30 minutes.

Cut each Shanghai cabbage lengthways in half and neatly trim the leaves. Wash and dry the leaves and stalks.

Heat 2 tablespoons of the oil in a small frying pan until just moderately hot and sauté the ginger and garlic briefly before adding the marinated shiitake. Continue to sauté gently until the shiitake acquire a glaze, then add the oyster sauce just before stirring in the potato flour mixture. Simmer for a few more seconds.

Meanwhile, bring enough water to cover the cabbage to a brisk boil in a wok or saucepan with the salt. Put in the cabbage and bring the water back to the boil as quickly as possible. Boil for 30 seconds. Remove and drain.

Wipe the wok, add the remaining oil and heat to moderately hot. Add the cabbage and toss quickly with a little sugar and the rice wine.

Arrange the shiitake in a neat mound on the plate and surround with the Shanghai cabbage, tucking the leaves under the stalks.

Presented in 1998

Nasi kemuli

(Nonya wedding rice)

Serves 4–6

30 g (1 oz) lard, ghee or butter

2.5 cm (1 inch) piece of ginger, peeled and julienned

5 shallots, sliced

2 garlic cloves, minced

½ cup coriander seeds

1 cinnamon stick

5 whole cloves

5 cardamom pods

3 whole mace

2 star anise

1 litre (35 fl oz/4 cups) water

400 g (14 oz/2 cups) long-grain rice, washed and drained

1 teaspoon dark soy sauce

1 teaspoon salt

2 tablespoons sultanas

Heat the lard, ghee or butter in a frying pan and sauté the ginger, shallot and garlic over medium heat until fragrant, then remove from the heat.

Boil the coriander seeds, cinnamon stick, cloves, cardamom pods, mace, star anise and water until the liquid resembles black tea and is reduced to 625 ml (21½ fl oz/2½ cups). Strain and discard the spices but retain the water.

Return the spiced water to the pan, add the rice, soy sauce, salt and the fried ginger mixture and combine well.

Tip the mixture into a rice cooker and cook until the water has been absorbed and the rice is fluffy. Stir through the sultanas to serve.

From left: Carlo Cracco, Antonio Carluccio, Luisa Valazza, Dieter Mueller, Marcus Eaves, Thierry Marx, Diego Giglio, Heston Blumenthal, Alain Alders, Sat Bains, Shane Osborn, James Petrie, Philip Howard, Kyle Connaughton, Jean-Paul Jeunet.

Neil Perry

Presented in 2002

Sichuan pickled cucumber and shiitake mushrooms

Fills a 2 litre (70 fl oz) capacity jar

7 Lebanese (short) cucumbers, cut lengthways into quarters and halved crossways

65 g (2⅓ oz/½ cup) sea salt

250 ml (9 fl oz/1 cup) peanut oil

1 tablespoon Sichuan peppercorns

10 small hot red chillies

90 g (3¼ oz) sugar

100 ml (3½ fl oz) rice wine vinegar

50 ml (1¾ fl oz) light soy sauce

1 large knob of ginger, shredded

20 dried shiitake (Chinese) mushrooms, soaked and thinly sliced

Put the cucumber into a colander over a bowl and sprinkle with the salt, mixing well. Stand for 1 hour to draw out any bitter juices, then rinse well under cold running water and drain.

In a wok, heat the peanut oil until smoking, add the peppercorns and chillies and cook until blackened. Add the sugar, vinegar, soy sauce, ginger, mushrooms and, finally, the cucumber. Stir for 1–2 minutes.

Pack into a 2 litre (70 fl oz) capacity heatproof glass jar, allow to cool, then cover with the lid and leave for a day or two to mature before using.

Serve as a condiment with rice and meat — it is absolutely delicious with roasted duck, or as a pickle in a sandwich with ham or chicken.

Shane Delia

Presented in 2010

Clove and cardamom frozen pumpkin, tahina and candied nuts

Serves 10–12

Pumpkin

1 kg (2 lb 4 oz) sugar

1 litre (35 fl oz/4 cups) water

10 whole cloves

12 cardamom pods, smashed

2 vanilla beans, split and seeds scraped

1 Jap pumpkin (winter squash) (about 2 kg/4 lb 8 oz), peeled, quartered and deseeded

tahina, for drizzling

candied walnuts (see recipe below) and fresh unsprayed violets or nasturtiums (optional), to serve

Candied walnuts

200 g (7 oz) walnuts, chopped into small pieces

150 g (5½ oz) sugar

50 ml (1¾ fl oz) dark rum

To make the pumpkin, prepare a stock syrup with the sugar, water, cloves, cardamom pods and vanilla beans and seeds. Bring to the boil over high heat, then reduce the heat to low and simmer for 5 minutes. Add the pumpkin and simmer over low heat until soft but still holding its shape. Remove from the heat and transfer to a large container. Place in the fridge to chill, making sure the pumpkin is covered with the syrup.

Soak for at least 24 hours to allow the pumpkin to take on the flavour of the syrup. After 24 hours take the pumpkin out of the syrup and place in the freezer until solid.

When ready to serve, place plates in the freezer for 10 minutes prior to serving. Shave the pumpkin with a sharp knife and place on the frozen plates. Drizzle with the tahina and sprinkle with the candied walnuts and flowers, if using.

To make the candied walnuts, place the walnuts in a wide heavy-based saucepan over medium heat and warm the nuts. Add half the sugar and stir through the nuts. As this starts to caramelise, add the rest of the sugar. Once the nuts are coated and the sugar is a nice golden colour, stir in the rum (being cautious as the steam is hot). Mix in the rum until the nuts are fairly loose and not clumped together. Place on a silicone mat or baking paper-lined tray and allow to cool down and crisp up.

Once cold, place in an airtight container and use when needed.

Note: The pumpkin has to be frozen rock hard before you can shave it — this will take at least 12 hours in a really cold freezer.

MFWF is undeniably the premier event on our culinary calendar. It unites an already strong dining community and shows the world our combined strength, passion and diversity. SHANE DELIA, 2010

Swing in
Manchester Lane
Event, 2009.

Philippe Mouchel (photographed by Melanie Dunea
for the My Last Supper Exhibition, 2008).

Chapter five

Tastes from the Water

The Melbourne Food and Wine Festival has always provided fertile ground for fish lovers who have, in the past, been memorably treated to Sophie Grigson's pumpkin, haddock and lime soup; or Rick Stein, arguably the best known seafood cook in the West, putting his own spin on all things fishy down at Docklands. But of course there are a lot of home-grown cooks who know their way around aquatic and amphibious creatures, especially given the quality of fish in Australia, Melbourne's access to fine fishing grounds and the surprising number of good fishmongers all of which mean locals are always on the lookout for new things to do with the daily catch. Andrew McConnell's combination of Western Australian marron and rockfish braised with saffron and harissa oil wowed MasterClass in 2005, as did the Asian-inspired take on marron tails by Christine Manfield in 2001.

Presented in 1997

Cold roast salmon with baby beets, pomelo and citrus oil

Serves 4 as an entrée

Citrus oil

1 orange

1 lemon

1 lime

100 ml (3½ fl oz) olive oil

Salmon

1 tablespoon coriander seeds

1 teaspoon each of white, black and Sichuan peppercorns

½ teaspoon sea salt

600 g (1 lb 5 oz) piece salmon fillet (thick end), skin and pin-bones removed

1 tablespoon olive oil

Beet salad

1 bunch baby beetroot (beets), stems trimmed and leaves retained

1 bunch golden beetroot (beets)

citrus oil (see recipe above), for drizzling

sea salt and freshly ground black pepper

1 pomelo, segmented

To serve

4 sprigs chervil, leaves picked

4 sprigs coriander (cilantro), leaves picked

Citrus oil

Remove the zest from the citrus in strips, removing any white pith from the zest, then squeeze the fruit and reserve the juice for the dressing.

Place the olive oil in a small saucepan over low heat and heat until just warm. Add the zest and stand overnight. Strain and store the oil in a cool dark place for up to 1 month.

Salmon

Coarsely grind the whole spices using a mortar and pestle, then combine with the salt. Coat the salmon fillet in the spice mix on all sides. Heat the olive oil in a large heavy-based frying pan over high heat. Sear the salmon on all sides until golden but still rare in the middle. Remove from the pan, cool and refrigerate until required.

Beet salad

Place the beetroot in a roasting tray, drizzle with a little citrus oil and season to taste. Bake at 160°C (315°F/Gas 2–3) or until tender, then remove from the oven and allow to cool. Remove the outer skin.

Mix the beetroot with the pomelo segments and beetroot leaves in a salad bowl, dress with a balanced mix of the citrus oil and the reserved citrus juice to taste (about 2 parts oil to 1 part juice).

To serve

Place the beet salad on a plate, cut the salmon into 4 pieces, place on the salad and dress with some more of the citrus dressing. Scatter with the chervil and coriander and serve.

Regional World's Longest Lunch,
Kilcunda, 2010.

Martin Boetz

Presented in 2004

Hot and sour soup of ocean perch

Serves 6 as part of a shared meal

Soup

750 ml (26 fl oz/3 cups) white fish stock

3 kaffir lime leaves

1 stalk lemongrass, bruised

4 red bird's eye chillies

5 slices galangal, peeled

2 coriander (cilantro) roots, scraped and cleaned

130 ml (4¼ fl oz) fish sauce

50 g (1¾ oz) chilli jam
(see page 152)

30 ml (1 fl oz) oyster sauce

2 red Asian shallots, halved

6 oyster mushrooms, cut into bite-sized pieces

1 tomato, cut into bite-sized pieces

1 whole plate-sized (600–700 g/ 1 lb 5 oz–1 lb 9 oz) ocean perch or red snapper, cleaned

vegetable oil, for deep-frying

juice of 1 lime

30 g (1 oz) pak chi farang (long-leaf coriander), finely shredded

extra chilli jam, to serve with the soup

continued >

Bring the stock to a boil, then add the lime leaves, lemongrass, red bird's eye chillies, galangal, coriander roots, 100 ml (3½ fl oz) of the fish sauce, chilli jam, oyster sauce and halved red shallots. Reduce the heat and simmer for 2–3 minutes to infuse the flavours. Check the seasoning. The taste should be hot, sour and salty. Add the mushrooms and tomato. Simmer for another 3 minutes.

Score the fish and rub with the remaining fish sauce.

Heat the vegetable oil in a wok to 180°C (350°F) and gently lower the fish into the oil. If the fish is fully immersed, fry until golden brown, 6–7 minutes. If the fish is not fully immersed, be sure to turn the fish so that it cooks evenly. Remove and drain on paper towel.

Put the fish into a large serving bowl and pour over the hot soup. Squeeze in the juice of 1 lime and add most of the finely shredded coriander. Garnish with the remaining coriander leaves and serve with some extra chilli jam on the side.

Chilli jam

1.5 litres (52 fl oz) vegetable oil

300 g (10½ oz) thinly sliced
red onion

200 g (7 oz) garlic, finely minced

15 long red chillies

100 g (3½ oz) dried shrimp,
soaked in warm water for
10 minutes, then drained

100 g (3½ oz) piece of galangal,
peeled, sliced and dry-roasted

100 g (3½ oz) palm sugar
(jaggery), pounded

100 ml (3½ fl oz) fish sauce or
1 tablespoon sea salt

100 ml (3½ fl oz) tamarind pulp

Chilli jam

Heat the oil in a wok or heavy-based saucepan until just smoking. Fry the onion until it turns the colour of lightly stained pine. Strain through a fine-mesh sieve, setting the onion aside to drain. You are using the same oil for each of the fried components of this chilli jam, so you need to strain the oil well. Fry the garlic until a light golden colour, then remove. Fry the chillies for no more than 10 seconds as they burn quite quickly. Take them out when they are a deep red colour. Place the dried shrimp in the oil, moving them around occasionally for about 1 minute. Take out and drain on paper towel. Reserve the oil.

Add the galangal to the fried ingredients and make into a paste. You can make this into a paste in one of several ways:

1. pound using a large mortar and pestle
2. blend in a food processor
3. use a mincer attachment and mince the ingredients three times, then finish by blending in a food processor. This last method gives the best result.

Place the paste in a heavy-based saucepan, strain the reserved oil into the pan and stir to combine. Heat the mixture to a simmer, stirring continuously. When hot, add the palm sugar, fish sauce and tamarind. Stir to mix through and remove from the heat. The paste should have a rich, roasted, sweet, sour and salty taste. It is often used as a base to flavour other dishes. Makes about 1 cup. Store in an airtight container in the fridge. It keeps for a few months.

Sophie Grigson

Presented in 2004

Pumpkin, smoked haddock and lime soup

Serves 4–6

Pumpkin is the most "delicate" of the winter squash fraternity. In other words, it is bland and needs boosting if it is to be anything more than soothing. This combination with smoked haddock and energising lime makes a delicious soup, with plenty of life to it.

1 onion, chopped

1–2 fresh red chillies (depending on strength), deseeded and chopped

2.5 cm (1 inch) piece of ginger, peeled and chopped

500 g (1 lb 2 oz) peeled and deseeded pumpkin (or other winter squash), roughly chopped

1 bouquet garni (sprig of thyme, rosemary, parsley and a fresh bay leaf tied together with string)

2 tablespoons extra virgin olive oil

300 g (10½ oz) undyed smoked haddock fillet

salt and pepper

juice of 1½ limes

250 ml (9 fl oz/1 cup) coconut milk

finely grated zest of 1 lime

1 handful of chopped coriander (cilantro)

3 spring onions (scallions), thinly sliced

Mix the onion, chilli, ginger, pumpkin, bouquet garni and oil in a large saucepan. Sweat over low heat, covered, for 10 minutes, stirring once or twice.

Meanwhile, place the haddock in a shallow dish and cover with boiling water. Leave for 5 minutes, then pour the water off into a measuring jug. If necessary, add more water to bring the level up to 450 ml (15½ fl oz). Flake the haddock, discarding the skin and bones.

Add the flaked haddock to the pan, together with the soaking water, salt and pepper. Bring up to the boil, then reduce the heat and simmer for 5–8 minutes. Draw off the heat. Remove and discard the bouquet garni. Liquidise in two batches, then return to the pan with the lime juice and coconut milk. Reheat without boiling. Taste and adjust the seasoning. Serve sprinkled with the grated lime zest, coriander and spring onion.

Earthly Abundance —
The Dinner, Prahran Market, 2010.

Presented in 1996

Sautéed scallops with crispy eggplant and spicy tomato relish

Serves 4

This dish shows another taste alternative with basic ingredients. The sweetness of the scallops mixed with an almost bitter/burnt flavour from the frying works really well with the tomato and olive notes. For a quick basic vinaigrette, just mix a few drops of balsamic vinegar with some olive oil and season with salt and pepper.

1 eggplant (aubergine)

2–3 tablespoons plain (all-purpose) flour

1 teaspoon cayenne pepper

sea salt and freshly ground black pepper

vegetable oil, for deep-frying

1 cup spicy tomato relish
(see page 160)

6–8 black olives, pitted and finely diced

basic vinaigrette or extra virgin olive oil

½ teaspoon olive oil

25 g (1 oz) unsalted butter

12 large scallops, cleaned and trimmed

mixed green salad leaves, such as rocket (arugula), curly endive and baby spinach

continued >

Halve the eggplant lengthways and very thinly slice crossways. Mix the plain flour with the cayenne pepper and a pinch of salt. Sprinkle the flour over the eggplant and lightly dust off the excess. These can now be fried in hot oil until golden and crispy. Drain on paper towel and sprinkle with salt. The eggplant can be fried before cooking the scallops and will stay crispy and warm while you finish preparing the dish.

Warm the tomato relish.

Mix the black olives with a little vinaigrette or extra virgin olive oil.

Heat a frying pan until very hot but not smoking. Add a few drops of the olive oil and a little butter. Sit the scallops in the pan, in batches if necessary to keep the pan hot; if the pan is not hot enough, the scallops will simply begin to stew in their own juices, which will spoil their taste and texture. Once the scallops are golden brown on both sides, turn them out, season with salt and pepper (and repeat if you are cooking in batches). Each batch should only take 1–2 minutes.

Season the salad leaves and toss with a little extra virgin olive oil. Spoon the warm tomato relish into the centre of each plate, making a circular platform for the scallops. Spoon the black olive dressing around. Sit the scallops onto the relish and place the salad leaves in the centre. To finish the dish, simply arrange the fried eggplant on top.

Spicy tomato relish

85 ml (2¾ fl oz) olive oil

3 shallots or 1 onion, finely chopped

2 garlic cloves, crushed

a few sprigs basil, thyme and tarragon

900 g (2 lb) tomatoes, peeled and deseeded

2 tablespoons red wine vinegar

1 teaspoon caster (superfine) sugar

salt

2–3 drops of Tabasco sauce

Spicy tomato relish

Warm the olive oil in a frying pan over low heat and add the chopped shallots or onion, the garlic and herbs. It's best to leave the herbs as sprigs as these can then be easily removed at the end of cooking. Allow the shallots and herbs to cook gently for 4–5 minutes or until tender.

Cut the tomato flesh into 5 mm (¼ inch) dice and add to the pan. Have the pan on a very low heat, just lightly simmering, and cook for 35–45 minutes or until most of the liquid has evaporated — this will really depend on the water content of the tomatoes.

Add the wine vinegar and sugar and cook for a further 15 minutes. The tomatoes should have taken on an almost lumpy sauce texture; if the sauce is very thick, simply fold in a little more olive oil. Allow to cool until just warm, then season with salt and Tabasco. Makes about 2 cups. This sauce goes so well with seafood of all types. It's almost like eating a chunky, spicy tomato chutney. Once made, it can be stored in the refrigerator for up to 2 weeks.

Christine Manfield

Presented in 2001

Grilled freshwater marron tails with shaved coconut, ruby grapefruit and mint salad, and fried shallots

Serves 6

Coconut-lime dressing

50 ml (1¾ fl oz) sugar syrup

100 ml (3½ fl oz) lime juice, strained

100 ml (3½ fl oz) coconut vinegar

25 ml (¾ fl oz) fish sauce

¼ teaspoon freshly ground black pepper

few drops of sesame oil

25 ml (¾ fl oz) extra virgin olive oil

Marron

3 × 350 g (12 oz) live freshwater marron

chilli oil, for brushing

sea salt and freshly ground white pepper

continued >

To make the coconut-lime dressing, mix all the ingredients together. Taste and adjust the seasoning if necessary.

Blanch the marron in boiling water for 2 minutes and plunge into iced water to stop them cooking further. Remove the tail and claw meat from the shells. (Use the shells to make stock for another use.) Arrange the marron meat on a baking tray, then brush with the chilli oil and sprinkle with the salt and pepper. Cook under a hot grill (broiler) for 3 minutes or until the flesh turns white. Remove from the heat.

Shaved coconut, ruby grapefruit and mint salad

1 ruby grapefruit

1 small cucumber, thinly sliced

3 green onions, thinly sliced

½ cup shaved fresh coconut

2 tablespoons chopped mint

2 tablespoons coriander (cilantro) leaves

1 tablespoon Thai or holy basil leaves

4 kaffir lime leaves, finely shredded

finely grated zest of 1 kaffir lime

2 teaspoons pickled ginger, shredded

2 teaspoons green mango pickle

2 red bird's eye chillies, deseeded and minced

1 cup baby watercress leaves

To serve

2 tablespoons fried shallots

To make the shaved coconut, ruby grapefruit and mint salad, remove the skin from the grapefruit and cut the fruit into segments, then dice. Mix the grapefruit and the remaining ingredients with the coconut-lime dressing in a bowl.

To serve, cut the cooked marron into slices, then toss through the salad and mix well to combine. Arrange the salad on plates, then sprinkle over the fried shallots and serve immediately.

Paul Wilson

Presented in 2004

Almond and salt cod panna cotta

Makes 6–8

Panna cotta

The day before cooking, place the salt cod in a large container of cold water and refrigerate for 24 hours, changing the water four times. Sprinkle the white fish with the sea salt, cover and refrigerate overnight. This will lightly cure the fish. The following day, drain the salt cod and rinse the white fish.

Place the milk, almonds, garlic and salt cod in a heavy-based saucepan and simmer over low heat, without boiling, until the salt cod is just cooked. Do not boil rapidly otherwise the milk will split.

Remove the cod from the pan, then add the white fish and cook until just cooked. Remove the white fish, then strain the cooking liquid through a fine-mesh sieve, reserving 250 ml (9 fl oz/1 cup) of the milk and some of the garlic shavings and almonds. Allow the cod, white fish and milk to cool.

Soak the gelatine leaves in cold water until softened, then drain and squeeze out the excess water. Place 100 ml (3½ fl oz) of the cooled reserved milk in a small saucepan over low heat until hot but not boiling. Add the squeezed gelatine and stir until dissolved, then remove from the heat.

Remove any skin and bones from the fish, then place the cooled fish and reserved garlic and almonds in a food processor and process until a smooth paste forms. Add the remaining cooled milk and process to form a smooth liquid. Pass the mixture through a sieve, then stir in the gelatine mixture. Refrigerate until elastic and starting to set. Fold in the whipped cream and check the seasoning. Lightly spray six or eight 50–75 ml (1¾–2⅔ fl oz) capacity moulds with canola oil, pour in the mixture and refrigerate until set.

Panna cotta

125 g (4½ oz) salt cod

125 g (4½ oz) white fish (free from skin and bones), such as snapper or blue-eye trevalla

10 g (¼ oz) sea salt

500 ml (17 fl oz/2 cups) milk

75 g (2⅔ oz) toasted almonds

2 garlic cloves, shaved

3½ leaves titanium-strength gelatine

70 g (2¼ oz) lightly whipped cream

seasoning

Almond milk dressing

50 g (1¾ oz) crustless white bread

1½ garlic cloves

seasoning

75 g (2⅔ oz) blanched whole almonds

250 ml (9 fl oz/1 cup) milk

125 ml (4 fl oz/½ cup) apple juice

To serve

85 g (3 oz) peeled green seedless grapes

100 g (3½ oz) picked watercress sprigs

sliced peeled green apple

50 g (1¾ oz/½ cup) toasted flaked almonds

1 avocado, peeled and roughly sliced

Almond milk dressing

Remove the crusts from the bread, thinly slice the garlic and liquidise all the ingredients in a food processor or blender. Season, then pass through a fine chinois and chill. The dressing must be served very cold.

To serve

Dip the base of the panna cotta moulds in hot water for 30 seconds, run a warm knife around the edges and invert onto serving plates. Garnish with the peeled grapes, watercress, apple slices, toasted almonds and 3–5 avocado slices per serve. Spoon a little almond milk dressing over the panna cotta and serve.

Wine

Over the past 20 years, the Melbourne Food and Wine Festival has left Melbourne's wine buffs breathless, gob-smacked and starry-eyed with its line-up of names and labels that range from rock star to benchmark and everywhere in between. Gathering together a roll call of the innovators, the movers and shakers, the modernisers and traditionalists, plus the heads of some of the greatest wine houses in the world, the Festival's wine program has become an accurate, broad-ranging and articulate snapshot of what is happening in the world of wine at that moment.

The breadth of wine knowledge in Melbourne has been one of the Festival's great strengths, with people such as James Halliday, Max Allen, Patrick Walsh, Jeremy Oliver and Ben Edwards helping to steer the direction of Wine MasterClasses, and the various, often associated, Winemaker Dinners, tastings, forums and tours.

From very early on the Festival proved itself to be adept at attracting the talent behind some of the wine world's most intriguing trends, whether it was Paolo de Marchi, one of the young Italian winemakers who are challenging the DOC restrictions in Chianti, with his Super Tuscan wines, coming to discuss his philosophy at the Festival in 1996; a gathering of the best wines from Canada, Uruguay, Brazil, Argentina, Chile and the USA at the 2010 event United Wines of the Americas; or with 2011's gathering of more than 60 of the world's leading biodynamic vintners called Return to Terroir.

In 1995 the Festival scored a coup (thanks, in large part, to the reach of wine writer and maker James Halliday) when Comte Alexandre de Lur-Saluces from the French house of Château d'Yquem brought five vintages of the legendary Sauternes to Melbourne. Because of the expense of the wine the Comte brought with him (valued at around $40,000 according to Peter Clemenger who, legend has it, stored the wine under his bed for safe keeping) there was a $145 surcharge for the d'Yquem MasterClass.

At the finish of the sold-out session, it was announced that Alexandre had had such a good time in Melbourne that he was donating the wine and so all would get their money back. Scarcely a dry eye in the house, apparently.

The presence of names such as Aubert de Villaine from Domaine de la Romanée-Conti, Henri Krug or Marc and Michel Chapoutier from the famed Rhône Valley house was a tremendous honour. As Sylvia Johnson puts it, "We'd never had people such as this come to Melbourne before — they were like gods to the wine industry and the attendees."

But it wasn't just the grand old names attracting the crowd; the 1994 Festival featured Randall Grahm from California's Bonny Doon Vineyard, while in 2010 two of the hottest young producers from Barolo in Italy, Chiara Boschis and Giuseppe Vaira, set various pulses racing in their session, Piedmont Under the Microscope — The Babes of Barolo and Barbaresco.

Then there was, as wine writer Max Allen puts it, "the cathedral-like silent reverence as a standing-room-only crowd settled in to taste a line-up of 1990 burgundies from Domaine de la Romanée-Conti with Aubert de Villaine" or James Godfrey's unforgettable MasterClass looking at 100 years of Seppelt Para ports.

The Festival has also been a great champion of the Victorian wine industry right from the start, which is not so surprising given that one of the Festival's two original paid employees,

Pamela Bakes, came from a background in helping promote the industry.

There has been a major focus on Victorian wine in the MasterClasses and Winemaker Dinners all through the Festival's history but it was an event that started in 1998 and has been a hugely popular drawcard at every subsequent Festival that has really hammered home to the wider population just how exciting, diverse and unique the Victorian wine industry really is.

Cellar Door and Farm Gate, formerly Cellar Door at Southgate, held every year beside the Yarra River, started off by bringing together 36 wineries from across the state and now has more than 60 Victorian wineries involved, pouring more than 200 wines over the course of the two-day event. As with the World's Longest Lunch and the Hawkers' Market, Cellar Door and Farm Gate and other winemaking events (the Acqua Panna Global Wine Experience), have been popular with the wider community because they bring a relaxed, almost carnival atmosphere to proceedings with the chance to taste — and buy — a huge variety of wine and to talk with the people who made it. It has always been part of the Festival's mission to provide the world's best wine but in accessible relaxed ways, for the many interested novices who can feel somewhat intimidated at more formal wine events. The presence of classes such as How Not To Drink Wine Like a Wanker signals that they're taking the mission seriously.

From top left: Roberto Anselmi, Global Wine Experience; Return to Terroir, 2011 (top middle, top right and bottom right).

World's Longest Lunch,
Flemington Race Course,
William Angliss student briefing, 2008.

Philippe Mouchel

Presented in 1999

Pan-fried prawns enhanced with tomato and red capsicum chutney

Serves 4

Tomato and red capsicum chutney

100 g (3½ oz) diced onion

250 g (9 oz) diced peeled apple

1 diced red capsicum (pepper)

1 diced yellow capsicum (pepper)

150 g (5½ oz) soft brown sugar

1 teaspoon Dijon mustard

½ teaspoon paprika

½ teaspoon curry powder

pinch of cayenne pepper

2 garlic cloves

125 ml (4 fl oz/½ cup) white wine vinegar

180 g (6⅓ oz) diced peeled tomato

Prawns

12 green prawns (shrimp), peeled and deveined with tails intact

2 teaspoons curry powder

large pinch of ground cinnamon

salt and pepper

olive oil, for pan-frying

To serve

seasonal salad greens, to serve

To make the tomato and red capsicum chutney, in a saucepan, place the onion, apple, red and yellow capsicum and stir over medium heat with a wooden spatula for 4–5 minutes or until the capsicum starts to soften a little. Add the brown sugar, Dijon mustard, spices and garlic, then add the vinegar and simmer for 30 minutes. Finally add the tomato and simmer for a further 10 minutes. Leave to cool. The chutney will improve in flavour after 1 week. Store in the refrigerator.

Season the prawns with the curry powder, cinnamon and salt and pepper. In a non-stick frying pan over medium–high heat, lightly pan-fry the prawns in olive oil.

To serve, place a small bouquet of seasonal salad greens on each plate, place 3 prawns next to it, top with a spoonful of chutney and serve immediately.

Presented in 2006

Seared scallops with lentils and a tomato and herbes de Provence dressing

Serves 4

For the dressing, put 2 tablespoons of the olive oil and the garlic into a small saucepan and place over medium–high heat. As soon as the garlic begins to sizzle, add the tomato and herbes de Provence and simmer for 10–12 minutes or until well reduced and thick. Put the vinegar and sugar into another small pan and boil rapidly until reduced to 2 teaspoons. Stir into the tomato sauce, season to taste and set aside.

Bring a pan of well-salted water (1 teaspoon per 600 ml/21 fl oz) to the boil. Add the lentils and cook for 15–20 minutes or until tender. Drain well, return to the pan with ½ tablespoon of the olive oil and some salt and pepper, cover and keep warm.

Slice each scallop horizontally into 2 thinner discs, leaving the roe attached to one slice. Place in a shallow dish with the remaining 2 tablespoons of olive oil, season and toss together well.

To finish the tomato dressing, add the remaining extra virgin olive oil, the lemon juice and some salt to taste and heat through gently over very low heat.

Meanwhile, heat a dry, reliably non-stick frying pan over high heat until smoking hot. Lower the heat slightly, add 1 teaspoon of the remaining olive oil and half the scallop slices and sear them for 1 minute on each side until golden brown. Lift onto a plate and repeat with the rest.

Divide the lentils between four warmed plates and arrange the scallop slices alongside. Stir the chopped parsley and basil into the tomato dressing and spoon some over and around the scallops.

From *Rick Stein's French Odyssey: Over 100 New Recipes Inspired by the Flavours of France*, Rick Stein, BBC Books (2005). Reprinted with permission of the Random House Group Ltd.

Ingredients

100 g (3½ oz) Puy (tiny blue-green) lentils

50 ml (1¾ fl oz) olive oil

12–16 large scallops, roe on

sea salt and freshly ground black pepper

Dressing

140 ml (4⅔ fl oz) extra virgin olive oil

4 small garlic cloves, finely chopped

4 medium vine-ripened tomatoes, peeled, deseeded and chopped

large pinch of dried herbes de Provence (or ½ teaspoon chopped mixed rosemary and thyme)

2 tablespoons red wine vinegar

1 teaspoon caster (superfine) sugar

1 tablespoon freshly squeezed lemon juice

1 teaspoon mixed chopped parsley and basil

Fresh sardine fillets grilled with sesame and soy, and whole mushrooms baked with parmesan and wild thyme

Serves 4

Sardines

20 sardines, butterflied and deboned

1 teaspoon soy sauce

1 teaspoon sesame oil

60 ml (2 fl oz/¼ cup) extra virgin olive oil

freshly ground black pepper

Garnish

12 fresh cep (porcini) mushrooms

4 sprigs wild thyme

2 garlic cloves, very thinly sliced

4 shallots, very thinly sliced

8 hazelnuts, roasted, peeled and coarsely chopped

2 tablespoons hazelnut oil

2 tablespoons olive oil

100 g (3½ oz) parmesan, thickly shaved

80 ml (2½ fl oz/⅓ cup) vegetable stock

splash of white balsamic vinegar

To make the garnish, preheat the oven to 180°C (350°F/Gas 4). Lay a sheet of foil on a baking tray and place the whole mushrooms on it. Top the mushrooms with the thyme, garlic, shallot, hazelnuts, hazelnut oil, olive oil and shaved parmesan and pour the vegetable stock over. Cover with another sheet of foil, seal well and bake for 10 minutes.

To prepare the sardines, mix the fillets with the combined soy sauce, sesame oil and olive oil. Lay them on a baking tray and season with pepper. Set aside until ready to cook.

When the garnish is ready, remove from the oven, open the foil and place the mushrooms on each plate. Pour the cooking juices in a bowl and emulsify it with the vinegar.

Cook the sardines under a hot grill (broiler) and place them on the mushrooms. Spoon the mushroom juices over the dish and serve.

Presented in 2006

Fillets of John Dory with cucumber and Noilly Prat

Serves 4

To make the sauce, pour the fish stock and Noilly Prat into a saucepan and boil rapidly until reduced by three-quarters to about 180 ml (5¾ fl oz). Now add the cream and continue to boil for 2 minutes. Remove from the heat and set aside until ready to serve.

Peel the cucumber, then cut in half lengthways. Scoop out the seeds with a melon baller or teaspoon, then cut each half crossways into 1 cm (½ inch) thick slices.

Preheat the grill (broiler) to high. Melt the butter in a large heavy-based frying pan. Brush the John Dory fillets with a little of the butter, season on both sides with salt and a little ground black pepper. Place, skin side up, on a lightly greased baking tray and set aside.

Heat the remaining melted butter in the pan until foaming, add the prepared cucumber and cook over high heat for 1–2 minutes, shaking the pan every now and then, or until lightly coloured. Season with salt and a little ground white pepper and remove from the heat.

Grill (broil) the fillets of John Dory for 2–3 minutes for those from smaller fish, or 5 minutes for those from larger ones, or until the skin is lightly browned and the fish is just cooked through.

When the fish is ready, bring the sauce back to the boil and whisk in the chilled butter, a few pieces at a time. Season to taste with a little salt.

Place the fish fillets in the centre of four warmed plates. Spoon the cucumber alongside the fish and sprinkle with the basil. Spoon the sauce over the cucumber and around the edge of the plates and serve.

From Rick Stein's French Odyssey: Over 100 New Recipes Inspired by the Flavours of France, Rick Stein, BBC Books (2005). Reprinted with permission of the Random House Group Ltd.

1 cucumber

25 g (1 oz) unsalted butter

4 × 450 g (1 lb) or 2 × 750–900 g (1 lb 10 oz–2 lb) John Dory, filleted, skin on

sea salt and freshly ground black and white pepper

1 tablespoon finely shredded basil

Sauce

600 ml (21 fl oz) fish stock

150 ml (5 fl oz) Noilly Prat

50 ml (1¾ fl oz) double (thick) cream

20 g (¾ oz) chilled unsalted butter, cut into small pieces

Twilight Dining in the Vines, All Saints Estate, 2010.

Andrew McConnell

Presented in 2005

West Australian marron and rockfish bouillabaisse with saffron, harissa oil and Sardinian couscous

Serves 6

Bouillabaisse

1 crayfish head, discard gills and chop into large pieces

1 crab, discard gills and chop into large pieces

3 rockfish heads

100 ml (3½ fl oz) olive oil

1 carrot, chopped

1 leek, chopped

½ onion, chopped

2 sticks celery, chopped

50 ml (1¾ fl oz) brandy

100 ml (3½ fl oz) white wine

750 ml (26 fl oz/3 cups) water

500 ml (17 fl oz/2 cups) chicken stock

good pinch of saffron

1 sprig tarragon

1 fresh bay leaf

2 sprigs thyme

2 stalks parsley

continued >

Bouillabaisse

In a large stainless steel saucepan over high heat, sauté the crayfish head, crab and fish heads in 3 tablespoons of the olive oil.

In a separate saucepan, sauté the mirepoix (carrot, leek, onion and celery) in the remaining olive oil and add to the first pan.

Deglaze with the brandy followed by the white wine. Gently reduce the liquid by half.

Add the water and chicken stock, saffron and herbs. Bring to a simmer and gently cook for 45 minutes, skimming any scum that may surface.

Strain through a fine sieve and discard the solids. Keep the broth warm.

Sardinian couscous

½ cup large fregola (Italian dried pasta similar to couscous)

2 tablespoons finely diced carrot

2 tablespoons finely diced celery

olive oil, for tossing

Chermoula

15 g (½ oz) cumin seeds, lightly toasted

7 g coriander seeds, lightly toasted

12 g sweet paprika

7 g ground ginger

1 small garlic clove

1 tablespoon lemon juice

50 ml (1¾ fl oz) olive oil

¼ teaspoon freshly ground black pepper

¼ teaspoon salt

1 teaspoon red wine vinegar

¼ bunch coriander (cilantro), washed and half the roots discarded

Harissa oil

50 g (1¾ oz) harissa paste (shop purchased)

50 ml (1¾ fl oz) olive oil

Sardinian couscous

Drop the fregola into salted boiling water. Cook for 6 minutes (or longer if using jumbo couscous), then add the vegetables and cook for a further 2 minutes. The fregola should be *al dente*.

Drain and refresh the fregola and vegetables, then toss with a little oil. Set aside until needed.

Chermoula

Place the cumin and coriander seeds in a mortar and grind until fine. Place into a food processor with the remaining ingredients and process until ground into a paste.

Harissa oil

Combine the harissa and oil until smooth.

A festival that truly focuses on delivering the essence of multiple cultures through the exploration of its food ... BRAVO! MICHAEL PSILAKIS, 2010

Braise

3 large marron, halved through the head (lengthways)

2 tablespoons olive oil

3 large flathead fillets, halved

6 red mullet fillets

750 ml (26 fl oz/3 cups) bouillabaisse *(see page 177)*

500 g (1 lb 2 oz) mussels, degorged and debearded

200 g (7 oz) baby clams (vongole), degorged

1 heaped tablespoon chermoula *(see recipe opposite)*

To serve

1 red capsicum (pepper), roasted, skinned and diced

½ teaspoon finely grated orange zest

juice of ½ lemon

harissa oil *(see recipe opposite)*, for drizzling

chopped flat-leaf (Italian) parsley, to serve

Braise

In a large, deep-sided non-stick frying pan over medium–high heat, sauté the marron, flesh side down, in the olive oil until golden and barely cooked through. Remove from the pan and set aside.

Add the flathead and red mullet to the same pan and cook for a few minutes until lightly coloured and nearly cooked. Remove the flathead and mullet from the pan.

Add the bouillabaisse, mussels and clams to the same hot pan. Simmer the broth and remove the mussels and clams as they open, taste the broth and adjust the seasoning. Whisk in the chermoula.

To serve

Strain the braise into a large clean saucepan and add the cooked fregola, capsicum, orange zest and lemon juice to the strained liquid.

Return the seafood to the braise, bring to a simmer and cook for approximately 1 minute or until cooked. Taste the broth and adjust the seasoning. Arrange the seafood and broth on a deep platter. Drizzle with the harissa oil and add a little chopped parsley.

Nigella Lawson,
Theatre of Ideas 2011.

Chapter six

Women of the Kitchen

There's never been a shortage of women fronting MasterClass at the Melbourne Food and Wine Festival but 2011 was a special year for female cooks and chefs. As the program for that year said: "Ask any chef about their earliest influences and you can bet your shiny new Pacojet that mothers will crop up somewhere in the conversations. We're training the spotlight on women and giving it up for the defining role they play in how we eat and drink that often gets hidden behind the peacock-like displays of their male counterparts."

The 2011 MasterClass featured people such as Nigella Lawson, the power duo of Stephanie and Maggie, and the experimental brilliance of Elena Arzak. It was a stellar year but there's been plenty of other legendary women on stage, from Rose Levy Beranbaum, Rachel Allen, Rosa Mitchell and Madhur Jaffrey to Karen Martini, Philippa Sibley, Jill Dupleix, Valli Little, Alla Wolf-Tasker and Margaret Fulton, all of whom have taken to the MasterClass stage at some time since the Festival's earliest days. It's quite the collection of sisters cooking it for themselves.

From left to right: Rose Gray, Langham Melbourne MasterClass, 2007; Rachel Allen, Langham Melbourne MasterClass, 2011; Jill Dupleix; Gabrielle Hamilton; Maggie Beer, Hands-On MasterClass, 2011; Alla Wolf-Tasker, MasterClass, 2011.

Presented in 2003

Jump-in-the-pan chicken

Serves 4

This is an action dish, a simple sauté in the pan that creates its own lovely lemony sauce. The trick is to keep the pan moving, jiggling it over the heat to make the chicken "jump" and help the sauce emulsify. Serve with wilted spinach and mashed potato, rice or buttered noodles.

3 skinless chicken breasts (about 150 g/5½ oz each)

2 tablespoons plain (all-purpose) flour

sea salt and freshly ground black pepper

2 tablespoons olive oil

1 tablespoon butter

150 ml (5 fl oz) dry white wine

1 garlic clove, crushed

4 fresh bay leaves

2 tablespoons salted capers, rinsed

2 tablespoons lemon juice

2 tablespoons flat-leaf (Italian) parsley leaves

Place each chicken breast between two sheets of plastic wrap and use a meat mallet or pestle to bash flat — and I mean as thin as a coin, almost breaking it up. Tear the chicken into little rags with your fingers and toss lightly in the flour, salt and pepper.

Heat the olive oil and butter in a large, heavy-based or non-stick frying pan over high heat. When hot, add the chicken, a few pieces at a time, so they don't clump together. Instead of stirring, make the chicken jump in the pan by moving the pan rapidly over the heat, flipping the chicken until it is lightly golden.

Add the white wine, garlic, bay leaves and capers, jiggling the pan over medium heat as the wine bubbles away.

Add the lemon juice, parsley leaves, salt and pepper, jiggling the pan until the chicken is coated in a creamy lemon sauce. Serve immediately with mashed potato and wilted spinach if desired.

World's Longest Lunch, St Kilda Road, 2010.

Rosa Mitchell

Presented in 2011

Stuffed Sicilian beef roll

(Falsomagro)

Serves 8

1.5 kg (3 lb 5 oz) girello roast or a piece of beef shoulder, deboned by your butcher and flattened as much as possible so that you can easily roll it

2 tablespoons grated parmesan

5 slices mortadella

large leaves from ½ bunch English spinach

5–6 hard-boiled eggs, peeled but left whole

125 ml (4 fl oz/½ cup) olive oil

Sauce

60 ml (2 fl oz/¼ cup) olive oil

1 large onion, finely chopped

1 small stick celery, finely chopped

1 small carrot, finely chopped

2.5 kg (5 lb 8 oz) tinned chopped tomatoes or 2 litres (70 fl oz) tomato passata (puréed tomatoes)

2 fresh bay leaves

salt and pepper

To make the sauce, heat the oil in a large saucepan that is big enough to later hold all the meat. Cook the onion, celery and carrot over low heat until golden, then add the tomatoes or passata and bay leaves, season with salt and pepper and leave to simmer while you prepare the meat.

Lay the meat on a clean surface. Season with salt and pepper and sprinkle with the cheese.

Lay the slices of mortadella down the centre of the meat (it's okay if they overlap). Next lay the spinach leaves over the mortadella. Place the eggs in a single line down the centre of the meat. Season again with salt and pepper.

Now comes the tricky part: rolling it up. Start to roll from one long side, tying as you go with kitchen string at intervals of about 8 cm (3¼ inches). Make sure the ends are tied very tightly or you will lose the eggs.

Heat the oil in a large frying pan and brown the "falsomagro" on all sides, then add it to the sauce in the pan.

Cover the pan and cook over very low heat for 1–1½ hours, turning occasionally. When cooked, remove from the sauce and leave to cool slightly. Slice and place on a large serving plate. Spoon over the sauce to serve.

Easy soda focaccia

Makes 1 loaf

As this recipe uses no yeast, it is not, strictly speaking, a proper Italian focaccia, but a quirky Irish–Italian mix, using a soda bread recipe. It's very quick to make and is delicious covered with a host of additional ingredients (see the variations below).

450 g (1 lb/3 cups) plain (all-purpose) flour

1 teaspoon salt

1 teaspoon bicarbonate of soda (baking soda)

350–400 ml (12–14 fl oz) buttermilk or sour milk (*see Rachel's baking tip opposite*)

a good drizzle of olive oil, about 60–75 ml (2–2⅔ fl oz)

sea salt, such as Maldon, for sprinkling

Preheat the oven to 220°C (425°F/Gas 7). Brush the inside of a 33 cm × 23 cm (13 ×9 inch) Swiss roll (jelly roll) tin or roasting tin generously with olive oil.

Sift the dry ingredients into a large bowl and make a well in the centre. Pour most of the buttermilk in at once and, using one hand with your fingers outstretched like a claw, mix in the flour from the side of the bowl, adding more buttermilk if necessary. The dough should be softish, but not too wet and sticky. When it all comes together, turn it out onto a floured board and roll it out so that it will fit into the Swiss roll tin. Make dimples all over with your fingertips on the top of the dough, then drizzle generously with the olive oil. Sprinkle with the sea salt.

Bake for about 30 minutes or until the bread is nice and golden on the top and bottom. If the bread is a good golden colour and you don't want it to darken any more during cooking, reduce the oven temperature to 200°C (400°F/Gas 6) and continue to bake for the remaining time.

When the focaccia is cooked but still hot, drizzle just a little more olive oil over the top and allow to cool slightly before serving.

Variations

Red onion, olive and rosemary   Place chunks of a peeled red onion, cut first into 6 wedges lengthways, then half crossways, onto the raw dough (3 across and 4 down, so that there are 12 altogether), so that each "square" will have some of everything. Next to the red onion, place a pitted olive (press it down slightly) and a little sprig of rosemary. Finish with the drizzle of olive oil and a sprinkling of sea salt. Bake as opposite.

Gruyère and thyme leaf   Sprinkle 150 g (5½ oz) grated Gruyère cheese and 2 teaspoons of thyme leaves over the raw dough, then drizzle with just a little olive oil and sprinkle with sea salt. Bake as opposite.

Sun-dried tomato and basil   Add a small handful of sun-dried tomatoes, about 50 g (1¾ oz), roughly chopped, and 1 tablespoon of chopped or torn basil to the dry ingredients at the start. Continue as opposite.

Brown soda focaccia   Replace 150 g (5½ oz/1 cup) of the flour with wholemeal (whole-wheat) flour and continue as above.

Rachel's baking tip: To make your own sour milk, heat the milk gently until warmed, then remove from the heat and add the juice of ½ lemon. Leave at room temperature overnight. If you are allergic to dairy products, this recipe works well with soy or rice milk soured in this way too.

We had an incredible time — so amazing. The Festival was fabulous — so exciting with a wonderful variety of food and foodies alike ... I think it's safe to say we ate our way through the city. RACHEL ALLEN, 2011

Karen Martini

Presented in 2004

Black figs with Gorgonzola, honey and walnuts

Serves 6

10 large ripe black figs

1 lemon, halved

100 ml (3½ fl oz) extra virgin olive oil

75 g (2⅔ oz) Gorgonzola, at room temperature

75 g (2⅔ oz) ricotta

4 slices white sourdough loaf

2 handfuls of whole walnuts, toasted lightly and skins rubbed off

salt and pepper

100 ml (3½ fl oz) of your favourite honey

Slice the figs into 3–4 generous rings each and lightly season with a squeeze of the lemon and a little oil.

Remove any rind from the Gorgonzola and dice into small cubes. Place in a food processor and blitz until smooth. Add a touch of water, if necessary, then add the ricotta and purée until you have a smooth paste.

Toast the slices of sourdough until crisp. Drizzle the walnuts with a little oil and season.

For individual plating, place a couple of fig rounds on each plate, top with a little Gorgonzola paste. Top haphazardly with more fig rings, building height, then a little more Gorgonzola paste and more figs. Scatter over the walnuts and crushed-up crostini. Squeeze over some lemon juice, season with a grind of pepper, drizzle with the honey and serve. This can also be served on a big platter for feasting.

Note: You could add a couple of rocket (argula) leaves to make an entrée or leave as is and serve as a cheese or dessert course.

Edible Garden, City Square, 2010.

Rose Levy Beranbaum

Presented in 2004

Stud muffin

Makes an 18 cm diameter x 14 cm high (7 x 5½ inch) round loaf / about 1 kg (2 lb 4 oz)

This three-cheese bread looks like a soufflé that never falls. It was inspired by a recipe called torta di Pasqua, or Easter cake, from Perugia, by cookbook author Jane Freiman. When sliced, it reveals a crumb that is almost lacy, with many medium-sized pockets that become coated with melted Gruyère. My favourite part of this bread is the crispy bits of Gruyère that work their way to the outside of the dough and melt and brown on the crust, so I stud the top surface all over with extra little cubes of it before baking, hence its name.

Prosciutto is a traditional accompaniment, with thin slices laid on the bread to serve as an appetiser, but I've also discovered a combination that serves brilliantly as a cheese course: inch-thick strips of the bread spread with Époisses (a runny, pungent French cheese) and a glass of Burgundy. Eat this and swoon with pleasure!

This dough is very quick to mix in a food processor. It requires a long, slow rise, but the actual work involved is minimal.

Special equipment

You will need either a soufflé dish (measuring 1.8 litre/64 fl oz capacity and 18 cm diameter x 9 cm high/7 × 3½ inches) or a large coffee can (15 cm diameter ×15 cm high/6 × 6 inches), well greased.

Dough starter (sponge)

156 g unbleached plain (all-purpose) flour

3 g dried active yeast

185 ml (6 fl oz/¾ cup) water, at room temperature

Dough starter (sponge)

1. Make the dough starter: Place the flour, yeast and water in a bowl or in the bowl of an electric mixer and whisk until very smooth to incorporate air, about 2 minutes. The sponge will be the consistency of a thick batter. Scrape down the side of the bowl. Cover tightly with plastic wrap and ferment for 1–4 hours at room temperature.

Dough

56 g Parmigiano-Reggiano, cut into
2.5 cm (1 inch) or smaller chunks

56 g pecorino Romano, cut into
2.5 cm (1 inch) or smaller chunks

343 g unbleached plain
(all-purpose) flour

5 g dried active yeast

1 teaspoon salt

1½ teaspoons freshly ground black
pepper

1 quantity dough starter (sponge)
(see recipe opposite)

56 g unsalted butter,
softened

125 ml (4 fl oz/½ cup) cold water

1 large egg, cold

70 g Gruyère, cut into 5–6 mm
(¼ inch) dice, plus 2 tablespoons
extra

1 teaspoon lightly beaten egg,
for glazing

continued >

2. Mix the dough: You can use a food processor or an electric mixer.

If using a food processor, fit it with the metal blade. Process the parmesan and pecorino Romano cheeses until finely grated (powdery). Transfer to a bowl and switch to the dough blade.

In a medium bowl, whisk together all but a scant ¼ cup of the flour, the yeast, salt and black pepper. Empty it into the food processor and scrape the dough starter over the top. Add the butter.

In a measuring cup with a spout, whisk together the cold water and large egg. With the machine running, slowly pour the mixture into the feed tube. Stop the machine, add the grated parmesan and pecorino and process for about 15 seconds or until the mixture forms a soft, shaggy ball. If the dough does not form a ball, add some or all of the remaining flour, 1 tablespoon at a time, processing in 4-second bursts. The dough should feel slightly sticky.

If using an electric mixer, first grate the parmesan and pecorino cheeses with a hand grater. In a measuring cup with a spout, whisk together the water and large egg.

In a medium bowl, whisk together all but a scant ¼ cup of the flour, the yeast, salt and black pepper. Sprinkle this mixture over the dough starter.

Add the softened butter and mix with the dough hook on low speed (setting 2 if using a KitchenAid), while gradually adding the water–egg mixture until the flour is moistened, about 1 minute. Add the parmesan and pecorino cheeses, increase the speed to medium (setting 4 on a KitchenAid), and knead the dough for 5 minutes or until elastic and bouncy. The dough should be slightly sticky. If it does not pull away from the bowl, beat in some or all of the remaining flour, 1 tablespoon at a time.

Tip the dough out of the food processor or electric mixer onto a lightly floured work surface and flatten it into a rectangle. Press ½ cup of the Gruyère cubes onto the dough, roll it up, and knead it to incorporate evenly. The dough will weigh 1050–1060 g.

3. Let the dough rise: Place the dough into a 1.8 litre (64 fl oz) capacity dough-rising container or bowl, lightly greased with cooking spray or oil. Push down the dough and lightly spray or oil the top. Cover the container with a lid or plastic wrap. With a piece of tape, mark on the side of the container at approximately where double the height of the dough would be. Refrigerate the dough. Allow it to chill for at least 8 hours or up to 2 days to firm and ripen (develop flavour). Pat it down two or three times after the first hour or two or until it stops rising — once the dough is cold, it will stop rising.

4. Shape the dough and let it rise again: Turn the dough out onto a work surface and knead it lightly. Round it into a ball. Push it down into the prepared mould; it will fill the soufflé dish or the coffee can half-full. Cover it lightly with a piece of baking paper and let it rise in a warm area about 27°C (80°F) or until almost tripled in size, 3–4 hours. (To reduce the rising time to 2 hours, place it in a proofer without water.) The centre should be at least ½ inch, preferably 1 inch, above the top of the dish or can.

5. Preheat the oven: Have an oven shelf at the lowest level and place a baking stone or baking sheet lined with foil on it before preheating to 180°C (350°F/Gas 4).

6. Glaze, stud, and bake the bread: Brush the surface of the dough with the lightly beaten egg, being careful not to brush the top of the dish or can, which would impede rising. Gently insert the remaining 2 tablespoons of Gruyère cubes into the dough using a chopstick — first gently twist the chopstick into the dough to make a shallow hole, then use the chopstick to push in a cheese cube; it should still be visible.

   Place the dish or can on the hot stone or baking sheet. Bake for 45–50 minutes or until the bread is golden and a skewer inserted in the middle comes out clean (an instant-read thermometer inserted into the centre should read about 88°C/190°F).

7. Cool and unmould the bread: Remove the dish or can from the oven and set it on a wire rack for 30 minutes. With the tip of a sharp knife, loosen the sides of the bread where the cheese may have crusted on it and unmould the bread onto its side onto a soft pillow (covered with a piece of plastic wrap to keep it clean) on the counter to finish cooling. This will prevent the soft fragile sides from collapsing. Turn it a few times to speed cooling, but always leave it on its side. It will take about 1 hour to cool completely.

Ultimate flavour variation: For the best flavour development, in step 1, allow the dough starter to ferment for 1 hour at room temperature, then refrigerate for 8–24 hours. If using the electric mixer method, remove it from the refrigerator 30 minutes before mixing.

Pointers for success: The bread stays moist and soft for 2 days but is great lightly toasted or heated for 3–4 minutes in a 200°C (400°F/Gas 6) oven to re-melt the cheese.

Presented in 2003

Little egg and ham pies

Makes 12

Preheat the oven to 180°C (350°F/Gas 4).

2 teaspoons olive oil or butter	

2 teaspoons olive oil or butter

12 thin slices ham, bacon or pancetta

12 large free-range eggs

sea salt and freshly ground black pepper

flat-leaf (Italian) parsley, plus extra to serve

30 g (1 oz/¼ cup) grated parmesan

Lightly oil or butter each mould of a large-hole muffin tray. Line each mould with a slice of ham, letting it flop out at the top (or run a slice of bacon around the inside), then break an egg into each hollow. Scatter with sea salt, pepper, parsley and grated parmesan.

Bake for 18–20 minutes — the egg should be just set and starting to shrink away from the sides and the ham should be crisp. Remove from the oven and leave to cool for 5 minutes. Run a knife around each mould to loosen. Top with a little parsley and serve hot for dinner, warm for brunch, or at room temperature in a school lunchbox or picnic hamper.

Loretta Sartori

Presented in 2004

Chocolate and honeyed fig tart

Makes a 20 cm (8 inch) diameter tart

Chocolate shortcrust pastry

140 g (5 oz) unsalted butter, softened

80 g (2¾ oz) icing (confectioner's) sugar

1 egg (55 g/2 oz)

130 g (4⅔ oz) plain (all-purpose) flour

25 g (1 oz) cocoa powder

Honeyed fig layer

20 g (¾ oz) unsalted butter

6 medium ripe figs, halved

50 g (1¾ oz) honey

2 g ground cinnamon

Chocolate shortcrust pastry

Using an electric mixer, cream the butter and icing sugar until pale. Add the egg and continue mixing. Sieve the flour and cocoa together, add to the butter mixture and stir until the pastry just comes together. Wrap the pastry in plastic wrap and refrigerate for 1 hour before using.

Honeyed fig layer

In a frying pan, melt the butter, add the figs and then the honey and cinnamon. Toss over high heat until the fruit begins to soften. Transfer to a plate and set aside to cool.

Filling

400 ml (14 fl oz) pouring (single) cream (35% fat)

½ vanilla bean, split and seeds scraped

2 eggs (55 g/2 oz each)

1 egg yolk

60 g (2¼ oz) caster (superfine) sugar

Chocolate glaze

150 ml (5 fl oz) pouring (single) cream (35% fat)

100 g (3½ oz) dark bitter chocolate, chopped

Filling

Bring the cream and vanilla bean and seeds to boiling point in a saucepan. Meanwhile, combine the eggs, egg yolk and sugar. Gradually pour the boiled cream over the egg mixture while continually stirring. Set aside until ready to assemble the tart.

Preheat the oven to 180°C (350°F/Gas 4).

Roll out the pastry on a lightly floured work surface to 3–4 mm (⅛–¼ inch) thick and use to line a 20 cm (8 inch) diameter tart tin with 4 cm (1½ inch) sides and a removable base. Refrigerate for 30 minutes.

Line the pastry case with baking paper, foil and weights and blind bake for about 30 minutes to cook the tart case thoroughly. Remove the weights, foil and paper. Remove from the oven and reduce the temperature to 165°C (320°F/Gas 2–3).

Nestle the fig halves into the tart case and pour over the juices. Remove the vanilla bean from the filling, then pour over the figs and bake for up to 1 hour or until set. Remove from the oven and stand until cool.

Chocolate glaze

Boil the cream and pour over the chopped chocolate. Stir gently until dissolved. Pour over the surface of the cooled tart. Refrigerate for 30 minutes or until the glaze is set. Serve the tart at room temperature.

Sizzle, Federation Square, 2008.

Melbourne

The Melbourne Food and Wine Festival's success comes from its innate understanding of the food and wine culture of Melbourne. The Festival is fine-tuned to the city's obsessions, shines a light on the industry professionals, and feeds Melburnians' thirst and hunger for the next big thing by providing a taste of the wider world. It truly projects a distinct sense of place.

A combination of good planning and good luck have led to the situation in Melbourne where the Festival still sticks to the original brief to "play to the Melburnians". Those running the Festival, past and present, have all been fired with the same belief that in a town that's home to 140 different cultures and more than 3,000 restaurants representing more than 70 cuisines, there is more than enough good stuff to attract a crowd.

From the earliest days of the Festival, Melbourne's impressive collection of produce markets has played a central role in the festivities. At the inaugural 1993 event, the Queen Victoria Market hosted both a breakfast and the first ever Hawkers' Market. There have been tours of the Footscray and Dandenong markets, lavish candlelit dinners among produce-laden stalls, and food and wine writers' forums held at the Prahran Market (now also home to the Festival HQ) and "Walking, Talking, Tasting Tours" of Melbourne's seven produce markets.

The Festival — in tandem with the hospitality industry of the city — has shown itself to have a certain genius for staging events in landmark and iconic locations around the city. This started, of course, with the first World's Longest Lunch at the MCG that set something of a benchmark and a tone for future Festivals.

There was the Breakfast Around the Tan, a massively complicated but much-loved event, first staged in 1998, which saw a progressive breakfast being served around the 3.7 kilometres former horseriding (now jogging and walking) track that follows the periphery of the Royal Botanic Gardens.

Or the still talked-about Donovans clambake, organised by restaurateurs and long-time Festival friends and collaborators Gail and Kevin Donovan, where crayfish and lobster were steamed under seaweed in a hole dug in the sand while guests, shaded by tent pavilions, were entertained by brass bands and marching girls. Or the Metlink Edible Garden that takes over the City Square, bristling with edible flowers, plants and trees, or the dinners and wine tastings that have taken place at the Melbourne Zoo, Crown Casino, Chinatown, Flemington Racecourse, Federation Square and, as part of a special feature of more recent years, a plethora of parties and drinks and tastings and barbecues down the city's laneways and up on its rooftops.

Melbourne's longstanding affair with cafe culture has also come under Festival scrutiny and, back in 2002, Celebrate the Bean, a one-day coffee festival at Southgate, shone an initial spotlight on the city's increasingly complicated, even fetish-like relation to coffee and the way it is grown, harvested, ground and brewed. This was reflected in the 2010 event Roasters' Week that saw seven of Melbourne's boutique roasters present a week of workshops, forums and tours — a sure sign of a city obsessed.

It's not the only obsession, as hugely popular events including Cellar Door and Farm Gate, formerly Cellar Door at Southgate that showcases the best of Victoria's wine and the ever-expanding roll call of Winemaker Dinners can attest. And then there is Restaurant Week — or Restaurant Express as it's now called — where Melbourne's best restaurants play host to the nearly 35,000 diners, who take advantage of a fixed-price lunch of two courses and a glass of wine — an affordable, accessible opportunity for many to experience restaurants they've heard and read about.

It seems that, over the years, the Festival has left no Melbourne icon untouched. For several years Melbourne's trams were part of the party with Tasting Trams travelling the City Circle route, plying travellers with small bite-sized snacks. Then there were the cooking demonstrations that took place in the window of the Myer department store and saw a roll call of great chefs and home cooks, strutting their culinary stuff to the crowds strolling past.

The Melbourne Food and Wine Festival has a talent for shining light into the corners of Melbourne and Victoria and, in doing so, lays the city and state open to discovery for visitors and its own inhabitants alike. In a city obsessed with wine and food it seems that there's always something new to taste.

Clockwise from top left: Cellar Door at Southgate, 2009; Flinders Street Station; Metlink Edible Garden, 2011; Wicked Sunday, Federation Square, 2009; World's Longest Lunch, Southbank, 2009; Crawl 'n' Bite, 2011.

Presented in 2004

Amaretti and strawberry tarts with balsamico

Makes 4

150 g (5½ oz) amaretti biscuits

80 g (2¾ oz) unsalted butter, melted, cooled, plus extra for greasing

200 g (7 oz) mascarpone

2 tablespoons icing (confectioner's) sugar, plus extra to dust

½ teaspoon vanilla extract

175 g (6 oz/1 cup) diced strawberries

125 ml (4 fl oz/½ cup) balsamic vinegar, simmered until reduced to 2 tablespoons

Preheat the oven to 170°C (325°F/Gas 3). Lightly grease four 8 cm diameter x 2 cm deep (3¾ x ¾ inch) loose-based tart tins.

Crush the biscuits in a food processor and combine with the melted butter. Press the mixture into the base and sides of the tart tins. Bake in the oven for 10 minutes, then allow to cool slightly before removing from the tins and allowing to cool completely.

Combine the mascarpone with 1½ tablespoons of the icing sugar and the vanilla extract until smooth.

Toss the strawberries with the remaining icing sugar. Fill the tarts with the mascarpone, pile on the strawberries, dust with icing sugar and drizzle with the reduced balsamic.

Loretta Sartori

Presented in 2003

Rhubarb nougatine

Serves 8–10

Sweet shortcrust pastry

Using an electric mixer fitted with a paddle attachment, cream the butter and sugar until pale. Add the egg and mix until absorbed. Stop the machine and add the flour, then mix on low speed until the ingredients are blended. Do not overmix. Wrap the pastry in plastic wrap and chill for at least 1 hour prior to use.

Roll out the pastry on a lightly floured work surface and use to line the base and sides of a 22 cm (8½ inch) diameter tart tin with a removable base. (Reserve the scraps for another use.) Refrigerate the pastry case for 30 minutes prior to baking.

Preheat the oven to 200°C (400°F/Gas 6). Line the pastry case with baking paper, foil and weights and blind bake for 15–20 minutes. Remove the weights, foil and paper. Reduce the oven to 180°C (350°F/ Gas 4).

Rhubarb layer

Wash the rhubarb and cut into 3 cm (1¼ inch) pieces. Rub the split and scraped vanilla bean into the sugar. Place the rhubarb into a sauté pan over high heat and cook until the fruit starts to sizzle. You may have to cook in batches if your pan is small — the rhubarb shouldn't stew. As the fruit starts to sizzle, sprinkle over the vanilla sugar. Once the sugar has dissolved and the fruit begins to soften, 4–5 minutes, remove from the heat. Set aside to cool.

Sweet shortcrust pastry

200 g (7 oz) unsalted butter, at room temperature

100 g (3½ oz) caster (superfine) sugar

1 egg (55 g/2 oz)

300 g (10½ oz/2 cups) plain (all-purpose) flour

Rhubarb layer

400 g (14 oz) rhubarb stalks (3 medium stalks)

½ vanilla bean, split and seeds scraped

50 g (1¾ oz) caster (superfine) sugar

Filling

70 g (2½ oz) unsalted butter, softened

50 g (1¾ oz) caster (superfine) sugar

100 g (3½ oz/1 cup) almond meal (ground almonds)

2 eggs (55 g/2 oz each)

Topping

90 g (3¼ oz) egg white, (from about 3 eggs)

80 g (2¾ oz) caster (superfine) sugar

100 g (3½ oz) flaked almonds, lightly toasted

Filling

Beat the butter and sugar in the bowl of an electric mixer until light and fluffy. Add the almond meal and finally the eggs, ensuring that the mixture is pale and lightly aerated. Spread the filling into the pre-cooked pastry case and cover with the cooled rhubarb.

Topping

Using an electric mixer, lightly whisk the egg white until foamy. Add the sugar and whisk for 1 minute. Remove from the mixer and fold through two-thirds of the flaked almonds, reserving the remainder to sprinkle on top of the tart.

Pour the topping over the tart, sprinkle with the remaining almonds and bake for 45 minutes or until golden and cooked through. This tart is best served at room temperature, or hot with vanilla ice cream.

Langham Melbourne MasterClass is all about inspiration, catching up with local heroes and global trends, going ooh-ah-how-amazing at what one chef may do, but then rushing home to make the simple, earth-to-table recipes of another. JILL DUPLEIX, 2010

My favourite thing about Melbourne Food and Wine Festival is meeting like-minded people who share gastronomic interest and passion. CHRISTINE MANFIELD, 2009

Christine Manfield

Presented in 1997

Valrhona chocolate jaffa mousse cake

Serves 12–14

Chocolate cake

Preheat the oven to 160°C (315°F/Gas 2–3). Line a greased 24 cm (9½ inch) round springform cake tin with baking paper.

Melt the chocolate and butter in a bain-marie. In a bowl, whisk the egg yolks and half the caster sugar until light and creamy. Add the orange zest.

Beat the egg whites in another bowl until stiff peaks form and, while still beating, slowly add the remaining sugar.

Mix the melted chocolate mixture into the egg yolk mixture, then gently fold through the stiff egg whites. Pour the cake mixture into the prepared tin. Cover the exposed surface with another sheet of baking paper to prevent a crust forming during the cooking process.

Bake for 20 minutes or until the centre is set. Check by inserting a skewer into the centre; if it comes out clean, the cake is cooked. Remove from the oven and sit the tin on a wire rack to cool.

Peel off the top layer of paper and any baking paper that may still be attached to the cake, but leave the cake in the tin. When the cake has totally cooled, wrap the entire cake and tin carefully in plastic wrap and store in the refrigerator until ready to use.

Chocolate ganache

Shave the chocolate finely with a knife and place in a bowl. Heat the cream and the liqueur together to simmering point and pour over the chocolate. Mix with a spoon until smooth.

Chocolate cake

200 g (7 oz) dark couverture chocolate

200 g (7 oz) unsalted butter

6 large eggs, separated

300 g (10½ oz) caster (superfine) sugar

finely grated zest of 1 orange

Chocolate ganache

250 g (9 oz) dark couverture chocolate

200 ml (7 fl oz) double (thick) cream (45% fat)

50 ml (1¾ fl oz) Cointreau or Grand Marnier liqueur

continued >

Chocolate jaffa mousse

200 ml (7 fl oz) milk

1 teaspoon finely grated orange zest

4 egg yolks

100 g (3½ oz) caster (superfine) sugar

50 ml (1¾ fl oz) strained freshly squeezed orange juice

150 g (5½ oz) dark couverture chocolate, chopped

4 g gelatine leaves

300 ml (10½ fl oz) double (thick) cream (45% fat), lightly whipped

To assemble

Valrhona cocoa powder, for dusting

Chocolate jaffa mousse

Heat the milk with the orange zest in a saucepan until simmering.

In a bowl, whisk the egg yolks and sugar until pale and creamy. Whisk in the orange juice. Pour over the hot milk, whisking constantly.

Melt the chocolate in a bowl over a bain-marie.

Soak the gelatine leaves in cold water until softened, squeeze out the water, add the gelatine to the egg mixture and cook over a bain-marie until it is the consistency of a custard. Strain the custard and discard the orange zest. Stir in the melted chocolate, remove the bowl from the heat and stir over ice until cooled. Fold in the whipped cream.

To assemble

Pour the chocolate ganache over the cake and let it set in the refrigerator.

Spread the chocolate jaffa mousse evenly over the cake and set in the refrigerator until the mousse is firm.

Remove the cake from the tin by releasing the collar of the tin. Dust the top with cocoa powder. Slice with a hot, wet knife to serve.

Presented in 2011

Coffee and walnut layer cake

Cuts into 8 generous slices

Neither of my grandmothers, nor indeed my mother, was a baker but this cake is nonetheless the cake of my childhood. When I was little, I used to make it for my younger sister's birthday every year, beating away vigorously with my bowl and wooden spoon. This, however, is a simplified version — everything just goes into the processor. The cake I made and ate when young was more milky coffee than espresso, but here I've bolstered it without consideration to my children. If that's your constituency or concern here, or if you yourself have a nostalgic longing for muted sweet comfort, replace the 1 tablespoon of instant espresso powder with 2 teaspoons of instant coffee granules dissolved in a tablespoonful of boiling water.

Sponge cake

50 g (1¾ oz) walnut pieces

225 g (8 oz) caster (superfine) sugar

225 g (8 oz) soft unsalted butter, plus extra for greasing

200 g (7 oz/1⅓ cups) plain (all-purpose) flour

1 tablespoon instant espresso powder

2½ teaspoons baking powder

½ teaspoon bicarbonate of soda (baking soda)

4 eggs

3–6 teaspoons milk

continued >

Sponge cake

Preheat the oven to 180°C (350°F/Gas 4). Butter two 20 cm (8 inch) sandwich cake tins and line the base of each with baking paper.

Put the walnut pieces and sugar into a food processor and blitz to a fine nutty powder. Add the butter, flour, espresso powder, baking powder, bicarbonate of soda and eggs and process to a smooth batter. Add the milk, pouring it down the funnel with the motor still running, or just pulsing, to loosen the cake mixture — it should be a soft, dropping consistency; add more milk if you need to. (If you are making this by hand, bash the nuts to a rubble-like powder with a rolling pin and mix with the dry ingredients, then cream the butter and sugar together, and beat in some dry ingredients and eggs alternately and, finally, the milk.)

Divide the mixture between the two lined tins and bake in the oven for 25 minutes or until the sponge has risen and feels springy to the touch. Cool the cakes in their tins on a wire rack for about 10 minutes, before turning out onto the wire rack and peeling off the baking paper.

When the sponges are cool, you can make the buttercream frosting.

Buttercream frosting

350 g (12 oz) icing (confectioner's) sugar

175 g (6 oz) unsalted butter, softened

2½ teaspoons instant espresso powder

25 g (1 oz) walnut halves, to decorate

Buttercream frosting

Pulse the icing sugar in the food processor until it is clump free, then add the butter and process to make a smooth icing.

Dissolve the instant espresso powder in 3 teaspoons of boiling water and add it while still hot to the processor, pulsing to blend into the buttercream. (If you are doing this by hand, sieve the icing sugar and beat it into the butter with a wooden spoon, then beat in the hot coffee liquid.)

Place 1 sponge cake upside down on a cake stand or serving plate. Spread with about half the frosting, then place on it the second sponge, right side up (so the two flat sides of the sponges meet in the middle) and cover the top with the remaining frosting in a ramshackle swirly pattern. This cake is all about old-fashioned, rustic charm, so don't worry unduly — however the frosting goes on is fine. Similarly, don't fret about some frosting oozing out around the middle — that's what makes it look so inviting.

Gently press the walnut halves into the top of the icing all around the edge of the cake, about 1 cm (½ inch) apart.

Make-ahead notes: The cake can be baked 1 day ahead and assembled before serving. Wrap the cake layers tightly in plastic wrap and store in an airtight container.

The buttercream frosting can be made 1 day ahead, covered with plastic wrap and refrigerated. Remove from the fridge 1–2 hours before needed to allow to come to room temperature, then beat briefly before use. The iced cake will keep for 2–3 days in an airtight container in a cool place.

Freezing notes: The uniced cake layers can be frozen on the day of baking, each wrapped in a double layer of plastic wrap and a layer of foil, for up to 3 months. Defrost for 3–4 hours on a wire rack at room temperature.

The frosting can be frozen separately in an airtight container for up to 3 months. Defrost overnight in the fridge, then bring to room temperature and beat briefly before use.

From *Kitchen: Recipes from the Heart of the Home*, Nigella Lawson, Chatto & Windus (2010). Reprinted with permission of the Random House Group Ltd.

To me the Melbourne Food and Wine Festival means fun.
What I love about Melbourne's food and wine culture
is that there is a lot of it. NIGELLA LAWSON. 2011

Presented in 1999

Soufflé of Valrhona Pur Caraibe with warm truffle centre and almond milk ice cream

Makes 8

Special equipment

8 metal dessert rings about
7 cm wide x 3.5 cm deep
(2¾ x 1⅓ inches)

canola oil spray

Truffle centre

170 g (6 oz) Valrhona Pur Caraibe
or best-quality bitter chocolate

115 ml (3¾ fl oz) thickened
(whipping) cream

Almond milk ice cream

1 litre (35 fl oz/4 cups) milk, plus
about 200 ml (7 fl oz) extra

200 g (7 oz) toasted flaked
almonds, plus extra to serve

300 g (10½ oz) caster (superfine)
sugar

350 ml (12 fl oz) cream

Line a baking tray with baking paper. Cut 8 separate strips of baking paper, 18 cm long x 6 cm wide (7 x 2½ inches). Spray the metal dessert rings with canola oil spray and line with the paper strips. Spray again and place on the baking tray.

Truffle centre

Finely grate the chocolate with the heel of a large knife and place in a metal bowl. Bring the cream to the boil and pour over the chocolate. Stir until smooth and shiny. Pour into a 20 cm × 15 cm (8 × 6 inch) baking paper-lined tray and freeze. Cut into 4 cm (1½ inch) squares and refrigerate until needed.

Almond milk ice cream

Bring the 1 litre (35 fl oz/4 cups) of milk to the boil and add the almonds. Remove from the heat and allow to infuse for 15 minutes. In a blender, whiz the infused milk and almonds until puréed. Line a conical strainer with 2 layers of muslin (cheesecloth) and pour in the almond milk. Allow to drip through until the almond left in the strainer appears pasty. Bring the corners of the muslin together and squeeze the remaining milk out of the paste. Measure the milk and add enough of the extra milk to make up to 1 litre (35 fl oz/4 cups) again.

Return the almond milk to the heat. Add the sugar and whisk until dissolved. Strain into a metal bowl and cool completely. Add the cream. Refrigerate. Churn in an ice-cream machine 30 minutes before needed.

Soufflé

225 g (8 oz) dark chocolate

50 g (1¾ oz) cold unsalted butter

200 g (7 oz) egg white
(about 7 eggs)

65 g (2⅓ oz) caster (superfine)
sugar

50 g (1¾ oz) egg yolk
(about 3 eggs)

Caramel sauce

150 g (5½ oz/⅔ cup) caster
(superfine) sugar

80 ml (2½ fl oz/⅓ cup) water

1 tablespoon Amaretto

Soufflé

Finely chop the chocolate, put in a metal bowl, and set over a saucepan of barely simmering water. Stir until melted, then add the butter. Turn off the heat but leave the bowl over the water to keep warm.

Start beating the egg white in an electric mixer. When they are white and just holding their shape, sprinkle in the sugar and continue beating until firm, but not snowy. Remove the chocolate from the heat and quickly stir in the yolks, then one-third of the whites. Fold in the remaining whites, taking care not to overmix.

Put the mixture into a piping bag. Carefully pipe approximately 1 tablespoon-sized blobs of soufflé mix into the dessert rings. Put a square of truffle on top of the soufflé mix, then pipe around and on top of the truffle until you reach the top of the rings (not the paper). Refrigerate the soufflés for 1 hour.

Caramel sauce

Place the sugar and 30 ml (1 fl oz) of the water in a small heavy-based saucepan over medium heat. Stir until the sugar dissolves, then simmer until a light caramel forms. Remove from the heat and pour in the remaining 50 ml (1¾ fl oz) of water, bit by bit. Take care, as it will splutter. Once the water is incorporated, add the Amaretto. Return to the heat and let it bubble for a minute. Allow to cool.

To serve

Churn the ice cream.

Preheat the oven to 180˚C (350˚F/Gas 4).

Place the soufflés in the oven and cook for 12 minutes.

While the soufflés are cooking, dribble a ring of the caramel sauce around the plates and put a little pile of flaked almonds where you will be placing the ice cream. Remove the soufflés from the rings by putting a wide palette knife under each one and gently lifting off the ring, leaving the paper in place. Transfer the soufflé to the plate, then peel off the paper. Using a spoon dipped in warm water, place an egg-shaped scoop of ice cream on top of the almonds and serve.

Chapter seven

Simple Comforts

The stages at MasterClass, filled with a roll call of the world's best chefs, have witnessed more than their fair share of culinary derring-do over the past two decades. And though that derring-do has included dramatic new technology, crazy ingredients and obscure cooking techniques, the power of simplicity, of a well-known homely dish done perfectly, has been similarly effective in capturing the imagination of audiences. Perhaps it is the achievability of Bill Granger's buttermilk pancakes or Fergus Henderson's chocolate ice cream. Or perhaps it is the spicy aromatic memories of Jill Dupleix's gingerbread or the comforting old-fashioned waft of Sophie Grigson's steamed apple, orange and ginger suet pudding. Whatever the reason, these are the simple comforting recipes that are in many ways the most satisfying to get just right. Nigella Lawson's spirited defence of home cooking at the 2011 Melbourne Food and Wine Festival and the overwhelming surge of positive reaction from the crowd that followed shows that, in a culinary world where whizbangery and celebritydom can sometimes get in the way of the food, there's no substitute for the everlasting appeal of simple comforts.

Sam and Sam Clark

Presented in 2007

Homemade cheese with pine nuts and honey

Makes about 1 kg (2 lb 4 oz)

Homemade cheese

Gently heat the milk to 32°C (90°F), then stir in the rennet. Transfer to a stainless-steel or glass bowl, cover with plastic wrap and leave in a warm place for 30 minutes or until the curd starts to separate from the whey and the milk sets.

Cut the curd into 3 cm (1¼ inch) squares with a thin knife to help release more of the whey. Cover and leave in a warm place for another hour.

When the cheese is firm enough to lift with a slotted spoon, carefully transfer to a colander set within a bowl. Refrigerate for at least 6 hours or until the curds and whey have fully separated and the cheese is firm. To speed up the process, cut the curd into smaller cubes.

To serve

Drizzle the honey liberally all over the cheese, followed by the pine nuts and a little mint if you wish. Soft fruit, such as apricots, raspberries, cherries, white peaches or nectarines, is also delicious with this.

Homemade cheese

2.4 litres (84 fl oz) full-cream organic milk (goat's or cow's)

½ teaspoon rennet

To serve

good-quality flower honey

100 g (3½ oz/⅔ cup) pine nuts, lightly toasted

1–2 tablespoons mint leaves (optional), finely chopped

Bill Granger

Presented in 2003

Bill's scrambled eggs

Serves 1

2 eggs

80 ml (2½ fl oz/⅓ cup) pouring (single) cream

pinch of salt

10 g (¼ oz) butter

Place the eggs, cream and salt in a bowl and whisk together.

Melt the butter in a non-stick frying pan over high heat, taking care not to burn the butter. Pour in the egg mixture and cook for 20 seconds or until gently set around the edge. Stir the egg mixture with a wooden spoon, gently bringing the egg mixture on the outside of the pan to the centre. The idea is to fold the eggs rather than to scramble them.

Leave to cook for 20 seconds longer and repeat the folding process. When the eggs are just set (remembering that they will continue cooking as they rest), turn out onto a plate and serve with hot toast.

Note: If you are making more than 2 serves of scrambled eggs, make sure you cook separate batches so as not to crowd the frying pan.

Rose Gray and Ruth Rogers

Presented in 2007

Summer ribollita

Serves 8

120 ml (3¾ fl oz) extra virgin olive oil

3 small red onions, chopped

1 celery heart, chopped, plus 3 tablespoons leaves

1 bulb garlic, peeled and sliced

500 g (1 lb 2 oz) silverbeet (Swiss chard), stalks sliced into large matchsticks and leaves left whole

3 tablespoons basil leaves

3 tablespoons marjoram leaves

4 tablespoons flat-leaf (Italian) parsley leaves

1 kg (2 lb 4 oz) fresh ripe roma (plum) tomatoes, peeled, deseeded and chopped

Maldon sea salt and freshly ground black pepper

300 g (10½ oz) fresh borage or spinach, tough stalks removed

500 g (1 lb 2 oz) podded borlotti (or cannellini) beans, cooked (see Note)

2 loaves ciabatta bread, stale if possible, crusts removed

In a large heavy-based saucepan, heat 60 ml (2 fl oz/¼ cup) of the olive oil, then add the onion and celery heart. Stir and cook gently until they soften and brown. Add the garlic and silverbeet stalks and continue to cook. When the garlic begins to colour, add half the basil, marjoram, parsley and celery leaves. Gently fry and stir together to combine the herbs, then add the chopped tomato. Season and simmer for 30 minutes — the tomatoes should reduce with the vegetables.

Separately, in another large saucepan full of boiling water with plenty of salt, blanch the silverbeet leaves, and then the spinach or borage. Drain, keeping the blanching water, and roughly chop.

Add the leaves to the vegetable and tomato mixture along with the cooked beans. Tear up the ciabatta into 3–5 cm (1¼–2 inch) lengths and add to the soup. Pour over some of the blanching water to moisten the bread and stir in the remaining herbs and celery leaves. Check for seasoning, then add the remaining 60 ml (2 fl oz/¼ cup) of olive oil. The consistency should be very thick.

Note: To cook fresh borlotti or cannellini beans, place the podded beans in a saucepan and cover well with water. Add 1 tomato, a handful of flat-leaf (Italian) parsley leaves and stalks and a few whole garlic cloves. Bring to the boil over medium–high heat, then reduce the heat to low and simmer gently for 45 minutes. Make sure the beans are covered with water at all times. Drain, then season.

Mario Batali

Presented in 2002

Bucatini all'amatriciana

Serves 4

340 g (11¾ oz) guanciale
(see Note), thinly sliced

2 garlic cloves, thinly sliced

1 red onion, halved and cut into
2 cm (¾ inch) thick slices

2 teaspoons hot chilli flakes,
or to taste

sea salt and freshly ground black
pepper, to taste

420 ml (14½ fl oz/1⅔ cups) basic
tomato sauce *(see recipe below)*

500 g (1 lb 2 oz) bucatini

1 small bunch flat-leaf (Italian)
parsley, leaves only

pecorino Romano cheese,
for grating

Basic tomato sauce

60 ml (2 fl oz/¼ cup) extra virgin
olive oil

1 red onion, cut into
1 cm (½ inch) dice

4 garlic cloves, thinly sliced

2 bunches thyme, leaves
picked and chopped, or
1 tablepsoon dried thyme

½ medium carrot, finely shredded

2 × 800 g (1 lb 12 oz) tins whole
tomatoes, crushed by hand and
juices reserved

salt, to taste

To make the tomato sauce, in a 4 litre (140 fl oz) capacity saucepan, heat the olive oil over medium heat. Add the onion and garlic and cook until soft and light golden brown, about 8–10 minutes. Add the thyme and carrot and cook for 5 minutes more or until the carrot is quite soft. Add the tomatoes and juice and bring to the boil, stirring often. Lower the heat and simmer for 20 minutes or until as thick as hot cereal. Season with salt and serve. This sauce keeps for 1 week in the refrigerator or up to 6 months in the freezer. Makes about 1.25 litres (44 fl oz).

Bring 6 litres (210 fl oz) of water to the boil and add 2 tablespoons of salt.

Working in batches, place the guanciale slices in a 35–40 cm (14–16 inch) sauté pan in a single layer and cook over medium–low heat until most of the fat has been rendered from the meat, turning occasionally and pouring off the fat to a bowl when necessary. Remove the meat to a plate lined with paper towel and discard half the fat, leaving enough in the pan to coat the garlic, onion and chilli flakes that you will add.

Return the guanciale to the pan with the garlic, onion and chilli flakes and cook over medium–high heat for 5 minutes or until the onion, garlic and guanciale are light golden brown. Season to taste, add the 420 ml of tomato sauce, reduce the heat and simmer for 10 minutes.

Cook the bucatini in the boiling water according to the packet directions until *al dente*. Drain the pasta and add it to the simmering sauce. Add the parsley leaves, increase the heat to high and toss to coat. Divide the pasta among four warmed pasta bowls. Top with freshly grated pecorino cheese and serve immediately.

Note: Derived from the Italian word guancia meaning cheek, guanciale is cured pig's cheek, which is stronger in flavour than pancetta, yet more delicate in texture. Available from good Italian delicatessens.

George Calombaris

Presented in 2004

Rizogalo

(Rice pudding)

Serves 4

1 litre (35 fl oz/4 cups) full-cream
milk, plus 2 tablespoons extra

100 g (3½ oz/½ cup) long-grain
white rice, washed
(see Yia Yia's tips)

1 cinnamon stick

finely grated zest of ½ lemon

2 teaspoons cornflour (cornstarch)

2 egg yolks

125 g (4½ oz) sugar

1 teaspoon vanilla extract

1 teaspoon ground cinnamon,
to serve

Bring the 1 litre (35 fl oz/4 cups) of milk up to the boil. Add the washed rice, cinnamon stick and lemon zest. Simmer over medium heat for about 15 minutes or until the rice is cooked.

Meanwhile, in a small saucepan, whisk the extra cold milk, cornflour and egg yolks together and stir over low heat until slightly thickened, but do not boil, then remove from the heat.

When the rice is ready, add the egg yolk mixture, sugar and vanilla. Simmer over low heat, stirring for another 5 minutes.

Remove the mixture from the heat. Set aside to cool, remove the cinnamon stick and pour into four individual bowls. Refrigerate until ready to use. Sprinkle each bowl with the ground cinnamon before serving.

Yia Yia's (my grandma's) tips: Make sure your rice is washed well. Rice has one of the highest amounts of bacteria — even more when served cold. Serve with Greek coffee (not Turkish) and finish with ice-cold rosewater.

Presented in 2011

Handmade macaroni

Serves 6

As a child, special occasions were celebrated with handmade macaroni; the women would sit around the table and roll the dough with a long thin reed that normally grows around water — you can use a very thin knitting needle that is pointed at both ends. I remember my grandmother would plait three macaronis together and, if it was your birthday, you got to eat it. We don't make them as much these days, which is unfortunate because it was a lot of fun sitting around the table gossiping and laughing.

500 g (1 lb 2 oz) plain (all purpose) flour

5 eggs, beaten

pinch of salt

Place the flour in a mound and make a well in the centre. Add the eggs and the salt. With a fork, start beating the eggs and gradually mix some of the flour till it starts to thicken. Now, with your hands, mix it all together till you have a ball of dough. Knead for 10–15 minutes till it is elastic and smooth. If it is too wet, you can always add a little more flour.

Divide it in half and roll one half till you have a long sausage shape about 1.5 cm (⅝ inch) wide. When you have a long length of dough, cut it into 3 cm (1¼ inch) lengths. You have to work quickly as the pieces will dry, so only do a few at a time. Keep the rest of the dough under a damp cloth while you are rolling.

Lay out a clean cloth on a work surface to place the macaroni on as you make them. You will need a clean smooth surface to work on and a little flour to stop the dough from sticking. Place a knitting needle lengthways on top of a length of dough. Roll the needle backwards and forwards, working your hands away from the centre outwards. Gently pull the dough away from the knitting needle and place on the cloth. Keep rolling till you have finished all the dough.

Bring a pot of salted water to the boil, add the macaroni and cook for 2–5 minutes, depending on the size you have made. Serve with a ragù or simple tomato sauce and lots of grated parmesan. Have fun.

World's Longest Lunch, Royal Exhibition Building, Carlton Gardens, 2011.

World's Longest Lunch, Noojee, 2009

Beyond Melbourne

One of the major reasons for the strength and depth of Melbourne's food and wine culture is that the city is surrounded on all sides by regional areas that produce an amazing array of brilliant things to drink and eat. It has been one of the Melbourne Food and Wine Festival's major achievements that it has helped alert Melburnians to the fact of the many delicious drinkable and edible riches right on their doorstep through a constantly expanding regional program.

In the Festival's early days, however, most of the energy was centred on Melbourne, which had more to do with limited resources than lack of interest. But it was also the case that Victoria's regions in the early 1990s did not have the distinct identities they have now. There was no coherent plan to promote regional wine and food tourism and city slickers were mostly unaware of what the countryside had to offer in terms of food and wine. In some cases the lack of greater awareness of all the good stuff in Victoria was partly due to the producers themselves who, having little to compare themselves with or opportunity to see what others were doing, were not aware of how good, even special, the food they were growing was. The Festival helped to promote events in regional Victoria, bringing the regions into the city by way of showcases, workshops, markets and dinners.

Aside from the Winemaker Dinners in the first couple of Festivals, the initial regional events consisted of balloon-ride-over-the-vineyard or drink-some-wine-and-listen-to-some-jazz type events. But then in 1998, the first of the Regional Producers Showcases and the Regional Food and Wine Tourism Workshops were organised which brought together small and artisan producers from across the state. Sylvia Johnson said it was remarkable to "see the small growers from all around Victoria coming together for the first time and coming to the realisation that they were not alone and, together, they had a lot to offer".

On the back of that discovery people such as Suzanne Halliday, wife of wine writer and Festival friend James, and dedicated spruiker of the Yarra Valley, championed the cause of the regions, helping to bring regionally specific produce to both the Festival and to Victoria through farmers' markets. In this way, people in the city — and in the regional areas where these markets began sprouting both in and out of Festival time — could access both the product and producer.

Then there were people such as George Biron, who every year runs a program of themed events from his farm in Deans Marsh, covering everything from wild food to the legacy of Elizabeth David. Or Alla Wolf-Tasker, a tireless worker for the regional cause that she embodies at her renowned Daylesford restaurant (and constant Festival venue), Lake House. Or Stefano de Pieri, a long-time and enthusiastic Festival participant, who has given the agricultural richness of Mildura a permanent place on the regional-produce map.

The level of interest and the size of the crowds that regional gatherings run by these people generated gave different regions the confidence to hold their own events during the Festival. For example, in 2005 Fruits of Our Labour shone the spotlight on the food and wine (especially pinot noir) of the Mornington Peninsula, and the Yarra Valley was the host of a series of Slow Food workshops that focused on the making of cheese, pasta, preserves and cured meat.

Of course, the event that really brought city and regions together symbolically was the World's Longest Lunch. After the first three Lunches had proved to be so successful in Melbourne, the decision was made to extend the lunches into the country as a way of promoting tourism to the regions. Now there are 25-plus Long Lunches held throughout Victoria in botanic gardens, on the foreshore of Port Phillip Bay, on wharfs and bridges, in showgrounds and wineries and on Avenues of Honour. There are lunches in the Grampians, the Yarra Valley and Dandenong Ranges, along the Murray River, on the Mornington and Bellarine peninsulas, along the Great Ocean Road, in the Macedon ranges and up in the High Country.

Working with the many dedicated people, including Wolf-Tasker, Biron, Halliday, Patrizia Simone, de Pieri and Dur-e Dara, who push the regional cause all year round, the Festival has been able to bring the message to a greater, food-savvy section of the population. And in doing so they have forged links that make the Festival feel as if it belongs not just to the capital but to the entire state.

Clockwise from top left: Adundance Dining, 2010; Regional World's Longest Lunch, 2007; Regional Produce, 2009; World's Longest Lunch, North East Valley, 2011; Abundance Dining, 2010 (bottom centre and left).

Presented in 2005

Tarte aux pommes à la Tatin

(Caramelised apple tart, caramel sauce and homemade vanilla ice cream)

Serves 6

200 g (7 oz) block puff pastry
4 golden delicious apples
90 g (3¼ oz) caster (superfine) sugar
30 g (1 oz) unsalted butter
30 ml (1 fl oz) Calvados *(see Note)*
vanilla ice cream *(see recipe opposite)*
100 ml (3½ fl oz) caramel Calvados *(see recipe opposite)*

Preheat the oven to 190°C (375°F/Gas 5).

Roll the pastry on a lightly floured work surface to 5 mm (¼ inch) thick. Using a 12 cm (4½ inch) round cutter, cut out 6 discs. Place the pastry discs on a baking paper-lined baking tray. Crimp the edges with your fingertips, pressing firmly. Prick each disc with the tines of a fork to prevent the pastry from rising. Transfer to the refrigerator.

Cut the ends off each apple, then peel. Cut 3 cheeks off each apple, avoiding the core. Slice each apple cheek as thinly as possible. Fan these slices out on each puff pastry disc until only a small hole remains in the centre. Fill the hole with a 2.5 cm (1 inch) disc of apple.

Sprinkle the sugar onto each tart, place a dot of butter on top and cook in the oven for 20 minutes or until the apple is coloured. Add a splash of Calvados to each tart, then carefully flip using a fish slice. Cook for a further 5 minutes or until the base is golden.

Remove from the oven and place a tray weighed down with a saucepan on top of the tarts for 15 minutes. This will create a visual "wow factor". Remove the tray, then reheat the tarts in the oven for 5 minutes or until crisp and hot. Serve with the vanilla ice cream and caramel Calvados sauce.

Note: Calvados is a dry spirit made from distilled cider in Normandy, northern France.

Vanilla ice cream

2 vanilla beans

500 ml (17 fl oz/2 cups) milk

500 ml (17 fl oz/2 cups) thickened (whipping) cream

100 g (3½ oz) trimoline (see Note)

9 egg yolks

200 g (7 oz) sugar

Caramel Calvados sauce

110 g (3¾ oz/½ cup) caster (superfine) sugar

200 ml (7 fl oz) double (thick) cream

50 ml (1¾ fl oz) Calvados

Vanilla ice cream

Split the vanilla beans lengthways and with the back of a knife scrape the seeds into a medium heavy-based saucepan. Add the vanilla bean halves, milk, cream and trimoline and simmer for 1 minute.

In a mixing bowl, whisk the egg yolks and sugar until pale and thick.

Pour a quarter of the milk mixture into the egg yolk mixture and stir to combine. Pour this into the milk mixture and stir well. Place the saucepan over low heat and, using a wooden spoon, stir constantly until the mixture thickens slightly and coats the back of the spoon. Strain the crème anglaise through a fine sieve into a bowl over an ice bath. Set aside, stirring occasionally, for 20 minutes or until cold. Place in an ice-cream machine and, following the manufacturer's instructions, churn until frozen and smooth. Let the ice cream set firm in the freezer for 1 hour before serving. Makes about 1.75 litres (61 fl oz).

Note: Trimoline is an inverted sugar (sugar that has been treated so it won't crystallise and form lumps) used in confectionery and ice cream. Substitute the same quantity of liquid glucose.

Caramel Calvados sauce

Melt the sugar in a heavy-based saucepan over low heat for 3–4 minutes or until golden brown. Stir in the cream and reduce for 4–5 minutes or until thickened. Add the Calvados and bring to the boil. Remove from the heat, cool and store in an airtight container in the fridge for up to 2 weeks. Serve hot. Makes 1 cup.

From *My Vue*, Shannon Bennett, Simon & Schuster Australia Pty Ltd (2004) and features at Bistro Vue, Melbourne.

Presented in 1996

Neenish tarts

Makes 24

Sweet shortcrust pastry

Using an electric mixer fitted with a paddle attachment, cream the butter and sugar until pale. Add the egg and mix until absorbed. Stop the machine and add the flour, then mix on low speed until the ingredients are blended. Do not overmix. Wrap the pastry in plastic wrap and chill for at least 1 hour prior to use.

Divide the pastry in half and refrigerate or freeze one half for another use. Knead the dough lightly and roll out on a lightly floured surface to approximately 3 mm (⅛ inch) in thickness. Using a 5–6 cm (2–2½ inch) cutter, cut out rounds and line twenty-four 6 cm (2½ inch) tartlet tins with the pastry. Refrigerate the tartlet cases for 30 minutes prior to baking.

Preheat the oven to 180°C (350°F/Gas 4). Bake the tartlet cases for 12–15 minutes. The cases do not need to be lined and weighted down with rice (otherwise known as blind baking).

Sweet shortcrust pastry

200 g (7 oz) unsalted butter, at room temperature

100 g (3½ oz) caster (superfine) sugar

1 egg (55 g/2 oz)

300 g (10½ oz/2 cups) plain (all-purpose) flour

continued >

260 g (9¼ oz) caster (superfine) sugar

2 eggs (60 g/2¼ oz each)

400 g (14 oz) unsalted butter, at room temperature

raspberry jam

150 g (5½ oz) fondant icing (available from Greek delicatessens)

sugar syrup, for thinning (if needed)

pink food colouring

50 g (1¾ oz) dark chocolate, melted

Buttercream

Place 200 g (7 oz) of the sugar in a small heavy-based saucepan, cover with water and stir over low heat until the sugar dissolves. Bring to the boil and continue cooking to 120°C (235°F).

Meanwhile, using an electric mixer, whisk the eggs with the remaining 60 g (2¼ oz) of sugar. When the sugar syrup is at 120°C, slowly pour into the whisking egg. Continue whisking until cool, then gradually add the butter. At this stage, the butter may initially appear to curdle, however, with further whisking it will soon appear light and creamy. (You can enhance the buttercream with a splash of kirsch, if desired.)

Note: If you add the butter when the eggs are still warm, then you will have a heavy, greasy cream. If the butter is too cold, then the mixture will remain curdled. In this instance, carefully warm over hot water and re-whisk.

To assemble

Place a small amount of the raspberry jam into the baked tartlet cases. Add a dob of buttercream and smooth over using a palette knife. Allow the tartlets to set in the refrigerator or at room temperature.

Carefully heat the fondant in a small saucepan or over a bain-marie to blood temperature (35–40°C/95–104°F). If the fondant is still thick, soften with sugar syrup — do not heat further. Lightly tint the fondant with pink food colouring. Using a palette knife, cover half of each tartlet with pink fondant. When all the tartlets are completed, add some melted chocolate to the remaining fondant to colour it. Cover the remaining half of each tartlet with the chocolate fondant. Do not refrigerate. Neenish tarts will keep, in an airtight container at room temperature, for 6 days.

Presented in 2003

Bill's buttermilk pancakes with blackberry butter

Serves 6

Blackberry butter

130 g (4⅔ oz/1 cup) fresh or frozen blackberries

1½ tablespoons sugar

1 tablespoon lemon juice

125 g (4½ oz) unsalted butter, softened

Buttermilk pancakes

300 g (10½ oz/2 cups) plain (all-purpose) flour

3 teaspoons baking powder

pinch of salt

2 tablespoons sugar

2 eggs, lightly beaten

750 ml (26 fl oz/3 cups) buttermilk

75 g (2⅔ oz) unsalted butter, melted, plus extra to grease pan

maple syrup, to serve

Blackberry butter

To make the blackberry butter, place the berries, sugar and lemon juice in a saucepan over high heat and bring to the boil. Reduce the heat and simmer for 5 minutes or until syrupy. Remove from the heat and cool completely.

Place the butter in a bowl and use a wooden spoon to whip until light. Fold through the blackberry mixture to create a ripple effect. Spoon into one or more ramekins, cover and refrigerate until required.

Buttermilk pancakes

To make the buttermilk pancakes, sift the flour, baking powder, salt and sugar into a large bowl. Stir to combine. Add the eggs, buttermilk and melted butter. Whisk to combine (don't worry about lumps at this stage).

Brush a small portion of the extra butter in a medium non-stick frying pan over medium heat. Ladle 80 ml (2½ fl oz/⅓ cup) of batter into the pan. Cook for about 2 minutes until bubbles appear on the surface of the pancake. Turn the pancake and cook the other side for about 1 minute. Transfer to a plate and keep warm while cooking the remaining pancakes.

To serve, stack the pancakes on each plate, spread with the blackberry butter and serve with a jug of maple syrup.

Fergus Henderson

Presented in 2008

Chocolate ice cream

Makes 1 litre (35 fl oz/4 cups)

We finally did it, battling with the schizophrenic nature of chocolate — the sweetness going in one direction, the chocolate taste in another, plus the chalkiness of bitter chocolate. The battle was worthwhile and we now have the perfect chocolate ice cream.

Ice cream base

200 g (7 oz) plain dark chocolate (with at least 70% cocoa solids)

6 large egg yolks

115 g (4 oz) caster (superfine) sugar

500 ml (17 fl oz/2 cups) full-fat milk

50 ml (1¾ fl oz) double (thick) cream

40 g (1½ oz/⅓ cup) good-quality cocoa powder

Caramel

70 g (2½ oz) caster (superfine) sugar

75 ml (2⅓ fl oz) water

To make the ice-cream base, chop the chocolate into small pieces and place in a bowl set over a saucepan of simmering water, making sure the water doesn't touch the base of the bowl. Leave to melt. Put the egg yolks and caster sugar in a separate bowl and whisk with electric beaters for about 5 minutes or until the mixture is thick enough to leave a trail on the surface when the beaters are lifted. Place the milk, cream and cocoa powder in a heavy-based saucepan and bring slowly to the boil, whisking occasionally to prevent the cocoa powder sticking to the bottom of the saucepan. Pour it over the egg yolk mixture, whisking constantly to prevent curdling. Then return the mixture to the saucepan and add the melted chocolate. Cook over low heat for about 5–8 minutes or until the mixture thickens enough to coat the back of a wooden spoon, stirring constantly. Remove from the heat, pour into a bowl and set aside.

To make the caramel, place the sugar and water in a small, deep, heavy-based saucepan and bring slowly to the boil, stirring to dissolve the sugar. Raise the heat and simmer, without stirring, until a very dark caramel is achieved.

Remove the caramel from the heat and whisk into the ice-cream base a little at a time. Pour through a fine sieve into a plastic container, then cool down quickly in an ice bath (a large bowl filled with ice cubes is fine). Leave in the fridge for 2 days before churning in an ice-cream machine. Once churned, leave for 3–4 days before eating. I know this might prove difficult, but it does improve the flavour.

Presented in 2004

Steamed apple, orange and ginger suet pudding

Serves 4–6

Steamed suet puddings are among Britain's most important contributions to world harmony. I make them occasionally for French friends, who all laugh heartily at the concept until they come to the actual tasting. Only then do they begin to understand what an amazingly wonderful creation the steamed pud is. This particular steamed pudding would, I have no doubt, go down particularly well in France, but for the time being I'm keeping it firmly here.

I still haven't decided whether this is better made with cooking apples or eating apples — I probably need to try it out both ways a few more times before I can be sure ... Both have their merits, so try it with whichever you have to hand, or even a mixture of the two. Either way, it is the long, slow, moist cooking that melds the flavours together in an utterly heavenly manner, ready to ooze out as the suet crust is cut into.

Crust

225 g (8 oz/1½ cups) self-raising flour

pinch of salt

110 g (3¾ oz) suet, finely chopped or grated

equal quantities of milk and water mixed (about 25 ml/¾ fl oz of each)

a little butter, for greasing the bowl

To make the crust mix flour with the salt, then stir in the suet until roughly combined. Add enough milk and water to make a soft, but not sticky dough. Grease the inside of a 1.5 litre (52 fl oz) capacity pudding basin.

Roll the pastry out on a floured work surface to give a circle large enough to line the basin. Cut out about a quarter of it and set it aside to make the lid. Lower the rest of the pastry into the basin, pinch the cut sides together and press the pastry gently into place so that the basin is completely lined.

about 675 g (1 lb 8 oz) eating or
cooking apples, peeled, cored and
cut into chunks

finely grated zest of 1 orange

juice of 1 orange

1 chunk preserved (stem) ginger,
finely chopped

170–225 g (6–8 oz) caster
(superfine) sugar or
demerara (raw) sugar

To make the filling, mix the ingredients together, then pile into the lined basin. Roll out the remaining pastry to form a circle large enough to cover the basin. Lay over the top, and pinch the edges together all around to seal the filling right in cosily.

Take a sheet of foil, smear the centre with a little extra butter and make a pleat down the centre. Lay it over the basin and tie firmly into place. Loop the ends of the string over, catching one under the taut string on the other side of the basin, then tying the ends together to form a handle.

Stand the pudding in a close-fitting saucepan on a trivet and pour in enough boiling water to come about halfway up the sides. Place on the heat and adjust the temperature so that it simmers gently. Cover with the lid (or a dome of foil if necessary) and leave to bubble away happily for some 2–3 hours. Check regularly and top up the water level with more boiling water, as needed.

Presented in 1998

Gingerbread people

Makes about 25 biscuits, or 12 larger men and women

Gingerbread has been eaten in France since the eleventh century, when the Gingerbread Fair was first held in Paris. The local monks would shape it into little pigs and animal shapes to sell. In England, Queen Elizabeth I ordered little ginger cakes to be baked in the shape of her courtiers, creating the first gingerbread men. Feel free to make your own gingerbread men, women, children, animals, stars, trees or rounds.

115 g (4 oz) soft brown sugar

90 g (3¼ oz) butter

175 ml (5¾ fl oz) golden syrup

1 tablespoon ground cinnamon

1 tablespoon ground ginger

1 teaspoon freshly grated ginger

1 tablespoon bicarbonate of soda (baking soda)

500 g (1 lb 2 oz/3⅓ cups) plain (all-purpose) flour

pinch of salt

2 eggs, beaten

Combine the sugar, butter, golden syrup, ground cinnamon and ginger, and fresh ginger in a heavy-based saucepan over low heat and let it melt, stirring. Remove from the heat and cool for 2 minutes, then quickly stir in the bicarbonate of soda until light and fluffy.

Sift the flour and salt into a large bowl. Make a well in the centre, add the beaten eggs and gradually add the syrup mixture, stirring until all the flour is incorporated and you have a dough. Wrap the dough in plastic wrap and chill for 1 hour.

Preheat the oven to 180°C (350°F/Gas 4).

Roll out the dough thinly on a floured surface. Cut into the desired shapes and place on baking trays lined with baking paper. Bake for 10 minutes. Remove from the oven and leave on the tray for 5 minutes before cooling on a wire rack. Store in an airtight container.

Jude Blereau

Presented in 2011

A rustic tart of late-season plums

Serves 6–8

This is one of the simplest desserts to make, and one of the most delicious. It has lots of fruit and only a small amount of pastry.

To make the pastry, using a pastry cutter, cut the butter into the flour and sugar until it is incorporated into the flour, but still quite chunky. The chunks do need to be small, but it is quite okay if some of them are a little smaller than a kidney bean. If using a food processor, pulse one or two times or until ready and turn out into a bowl. Don't be tempted to add the water to the food processor as it is too easy to overwork the pastry.

Using a butter knife, begin to mix the cold water into the flour and butter. This is the step most people need to keep practising — you will never use the same amount of water twice as it depends on the freshness of the flour, the humidity on the day, the temperature and if any of your butter has melted. The idea is to add a small amount of water and begin to cut and mix it in with the knife. As you continue to add the water, little bit by little bit, you are cutting the wet bits into the dry bits, cutting, mixing and stirring. You use only as much water as you need. By cutting the wet dough into the dry bits, you avoid using too much water (another reason for tough pastry). Once all the mix looks moist, bring it together into a ball, DO NOT KNEAD OR PLAY WITH IT. Flatten the ball, wrap and chill long enough to take the softness out of the butter, about 20 minutes.

Preheat the oven to 200°C (400°F/Gas 6). Line a baking tray with baking paper.

Pastry

180 g (6¼ oz) cold unsalted butter, chopped

300 g (10½ oz/2 cups) unbleached plain (all-purpose) flour (wheat or spelt)

1½ tablespoons golden caster (superfine) sugar, plus extra for sprinkling

100–220 ml (3½–7⅔ fl oz) ice-cold water

continued >

Filling

1 kg (2 lb 4 oz) (measured with
stones in) plums

½ teaspoon ground cinnamon

1 teaspoon vanilla paste

1½–2 tablespoons raw sugar or
maple syrup (taste your
fruit first and see how sweet it is,
remembering there is sugar
in the pastry)

1½ tablespoons cornflour
(cornstarch) or flour

To make the filling, cut the plums into your desired size — halves or quarters depending on the size of the plums — and place in a bowl. Add the cinnamon, vanilla paste, sugar or maple syrup and cornflour and toss through gently.

Roll out the pastry to approximately a 30–35 cm (12–14 inch) diameter circle. Fold and move the pastry to the baking tray and unfold. Depending on the size of the tray, it may overhang the sides a little, which is fine. If the weather is very hot, you may need to give it a couple of minutes in the fridge.

To make the tart, the pastry should be chilled but not so firm that you can't fold the sides inward. Either arrange the prepared fruit in an attractive pattern, or simply pile it into the middle and gently spread to leave a border of approximately 8 cm (3¼ inches). Fold the pastry border over the fruit, peeling it from the paper underneath as you go. Sprinkle with a little extra golden caster sugar if desired. If required, trim the sides of the baking paper to fit the tray.

Bake for 15–20 minutes, then reduce the heat to 180°C (350°F/Gas 4) and bake for another 35 minutes or until the pastry is light golden and the juices are bubbling. Don't be worried if the juices look too watery, they will thicken as they cool a little.

Acknowledgements

A toast from the festival team

A great many individuals have contributed to the growth and success of Melbourne Food and Wine Festival over the past 20 years. We thank you for your time, your passion, your ideas, your hard work, your creative brilliance, your expertise, your resourcefulness, your laughter, your conversation and, of course, your world-class food and wine.

Without singling out individuals, we extend our heartfelt thanks to the following kindred lovers of good food and wine:

Victoria's restaurateurs, chefs, maître d's, sommeliers, waiters, cooks, food producers, winemakers, brewers, artisans, gardeners, bartenders, baristas, culinary communicators, wine commentators; valued sponsors, government and media partners; the Festival's founders, staff past and present, creative consultants and honorary committees and event review panels; interstate and international MasterClass alumni and host chef Anthony Ross; more than 100 Melbourne Food and Wine Festival Legends and honorary Legend, Peter Clemenger, the Festival's Founder and Patron; the Festival's suppliers and agencies, supportive industry bodies and an army of volunteers; our four official community partners; and a food and wine-obsessed Victorian community and the hundreds of thousands of visitors who join us for the Festival each March.

To each and every one of you, we toast!

The team at Melbourne Food and Wine Festival

Index

Page numbers in bold indicate recipes; page numbers in italics indicate photographs.

Published in 2012 by Murdoch Books Pty Limited

Murdoch Books Australia
Pier 8/9
23 Hickson Road
Millers Point NSW 2000
Phone: +61 (0) 2 8220 2000
Fax: +61 (0) 2 8220 2558
www.murdochbooks.com.au
info@murdochbooks.com.au

Murdoch Books UK Limited
Erico House, 6th Floor
93–99 Upper Richmond Road
Putney, London SW15 2TG
Phone: +44 (0) 20 8785 5995
Fax: +44 (0) 20 8785 5985
www.murdochbooks.co.uk
info@murdochbooks.co.uk

For Corporate Orders & Custom Publishing contact Noel Hammond,
National Business Development Manager, Murdoch Books Australia

Publishing Manager, Food: Anneka Manning
Publisher: Sally Webb
Project Manager: Laura Wilson
Copyeditor: Belinda So
Designer: Nikki Townsend
Food Photographer: Alicia Taylor; all recipes except pages specified below.
Food Stylist: Lee-Ann Blaylock
Food Editor: Christine Osmond
Home Economist: Caroline Jones
Production: Joan Beal

Introduction and narrative written by Michael Harden
Text © Murdoch Books Pty Limited 2012
Design © Murdoch Books Pty Limited 2012
Food photography © Alicia Taylor 2012. Except pages 82, 90, 106 courtesy of Melbourne Food and Wine Festival image library;
    page 84 copyright © Anson Smart 2011; page 100 courtesy of José López and Restaurant Arzak.

Front cover photograph by Alicia Taylor

Location and portrait photography provided courtesy of Melbourne Food and Wine Festival image library. Except page 14, Stephanie
    Alexander and Geoff Dobson photographed by Simon Schluter, courtesy of The Age, and photographs of Leo Pellegrini, Jonathon
    Gianfreda and Mietta O'Donnell courtesy of The Age; page 137, photographs of Jacques Reymond, Alla Wolf-Tasker and Shannon
    Bennett and page 149, photograph of Philippe Mouchel © Melanie Dunea/CPi. Photographs taken as part of the My Last Supper
    Exhibition, 2008, www.mylastsupper.com.

Every effort has been made to contact copyright holders. However, the publishers will be glad to rectify in future editions any inadvertent
omissions brought to their attention. The publisher and Melbourne Food and Wine Festival would like to thank all contributors for permission
to reproduce copyright material.

National Library of Australia Cataloguing-in-Publication Data

Title: Cooking with the World's Best: Celebrating 20 years of the
                              Melbourne Food and Wine Festival.
ISBN: 978-1-74266-511-5 (hbk.)
Notes: Includes bibliographical references and index.
Subjects: Melbourne Food and Wine Festival. Festivals — Victoria — Melbourne.
Dewey Number: 394.26099451
A catalogue record for this book is available from the British Library.

Printed by C & C Offset Printing Co. Ltd, China

Melbourne Food and Wine (MFW) is a non-profit organisation that runs the annual Melbourne Food and Wine Festival as a cultural
celebration and works with four key community partner organisations to provide support, exposure and guidance year-round. MFW will
proudly make a significant donation to each partner using the proceeds of this commemorative cookbook. These partners are StreetSmart,
Stephanie Alexander's Kitchen Garden Foundation (SAKGF), SecondBite and HEAT (Hospitality Employment and Training).

IMPORTANT: Those who might be at risk from the effects of salmonella poisoning (the elderly, pregnant women, young children and those
suffering from immune deficiency diseases) should consult their doctor with any concerns about eating raw eggs.

OVEN GUIDE: You may find cooking times vary depending on the oven you are using. For fan-forced ovens, as a general rule, set the oven
temperature to 20°C (35°F) lower than indicated in the recipe. We have used 20 ml (4 teaspoon) tablespoon measures. If you are using a
15 ml (3 teaspoon) tablespoon, for most recipes the difference won't be noticeable. However, for recipes using yeast, gelatine, baking powder,
bicarbonate of soda (baking soda), small amounts of flour and cornflour (cornstarch), add an extra teaspoon for each tablespoon specified.